It's A Wonderful Life

BASED O ~~~~~~ **ILM**

Original *ey*
Orch

SAMUEL FRENCH, INC.
45 WEST 25TH STREET   NEW YORK 10010
7623 SUNSET BOULEVARD HOLLYWOOD 90046
LONDON   TORONTO

IMPORTANT BILLING AND CREDIT REQUIREMENTS

All producers of IT'S A WONDERFUL LIFE *must* give credit to the Authors of the Work in all programs distributed in connection with performances of the Work, and in all instances in which the title of the Work appears for the purposes of advertising, publicizing or otherwise exploiting a production thereof; including, without limitation, to programs, souvenir books and playbills. The names of the Authors *must* also appear on a separate line in which no other matter appears, immediately following the title of the Work, and *must* be in size of type not less than 50% of the size of type used for the title of the Work. Billing *must* be substantially as follows:

(Name of Producer)
presents

IT'S A WONDERFUL LIFE
A New Musical
Based on the Frank Capra film and the original story by Philip Van Doren Stern, copyright 1944, 1958. Produced by special arrangement with Samuel French, Inc.

Book, Music and Lyrics by Thomas M. Sharkey

Original Piano Arrangements by Jack Sharkey
Orchestration and Vocal Arrangements by David J. Blackburn

iii

CHARACTERS

GEORGE BAILEY, a dreamer, a plodder, a man among men, and—as he sees it—a failure.

MARY HATCH BAILEY, the best thing that ever happened to George.

CLARENCE ODDBODY, George's guardian angel.

JOSEPH,* Clarence's boss and mentor.

UNCLE BILLY, a loving if sometimes foolish man.

MOTHER BAILEY, lovable, wise, and strong.

VIOLET BICK, a flirt, who loves George almost as much as Mary does.

HENRY POTTER,* the richest and meanest man in the county.

HARRY BAILEY, the brother who lives the life George might have led.

GOWER, an aging druggist.

BERT, a cop.

ERNIE, a cab driver.

ZUZU, George and Mary's daughter.

POTTER'S MAN,* who is both valet and goon.

TIME & PLACE

THE TIME is the 1930's and '40's.

THE PLACE is in, around, and *above* Bedford Falls, a small, working-class town in Upstate New York.

---

* Note: The actor playing the never-seen JOSEPH will usually double as POTTER'S MAN. The actor playing POTTER will usually double in some of the anonymous crowd scenes. The play is thus well-served with only 13 actors: nine male and four female.

MUSICAL NUMBERS

IT'S A WONDERFUL LIFE

ACT I

[Music #1: OVERTURE]

Immediately following Overture, MUSIC continuing, CURTAIN starts up on a partially lit stage and we hear:

[Music #2: SAVE HIM!]

ENSEMBLE.
SAVE HIM, SAVE HIM, SAVE HIM, SAVE
HIM...
MOTHER.
HELP HIM, FATHER!
ZUZU.
HELP MY DAD!
ENSEMBLE.
SAVE HIM! SAVE HIM!
HARRY.
HELP MY BROTHER!
UNCLE BILLY. *(Spoken.)* Help the lad!
ENSEMBLE.
SAVE HIM! SAVE HIM!
MARY.
WON'T YOU LET HIM KNOW—
GOD, I LOVE HIM SO!
ENSEMBLE.
SAVE HIM FROM THE RIVER'S SWELL!
SAVE HIM FROM THE SEXTON'S KNELL! ...

(THEY pause as a SPOT hits CLARENCE on a raised platform at L.** HE's an older man from an older time and terribly likable. HE is in some discomfort at the moment, however, blinking his reaction to the light's blinding force as HE looks about, lost.)

CLARENCE. *(Small, tentative, but on the beat.)* ... Hello?

(MUSIC is buttoned and we hear JOSEPH, who will remain off throughout.)

JOSEPH. *(Voice of God—almost.)* Ah, Clarence the clockmaker!

[Music #3: ARIA DI CLARENCE]

CLARENCE. *(Tries to see past the light, blinking.)* Joseph—is that you?
JOSEPH. I see you don't yet have your wings.
CLARENCE. No.
JOSEPH. No?
CLARENCE. Yes.
JOSEPH. Yes?
CLARENCE. True. *(Sings.)*
I HAVEN'T GOT MY WINGS
AND LOTS O' OTHER THINGS.
BUT WHAT'S A POOR ANGEL TO DO?

(Curtsies gently as HE finishes, causing JOSEPH, who likes him, to laugh.)

JOSEPH. *(Sobering.)* Clarence ... there's a man named George who needs your help tonight.
CLARENCE. Tonight?

** To avoid misunderstandings, all designations of "left" and "right" will be from the audience point of view.

JOSEPH. A good man but in trouble. About to quit the fight.

CLARENCE. (*Misunderstands, strikes a pugilistic pose.*) The *fight*?

JOSEPH. He's thinking of taking his *life*, Clarence.

CLARENCE. (*Sad, astonished.*) So close—(*Checks his gold pocket watch.*) to Christmas Day?

JOSEPH. But you can help.

CLARENCE. (*Immediately.*) I will! (*Then, lost.*) But how?

JOSEPH. Listen! Hear them pray.

[Music #3A: INCIDENTAL SAVE HIMS]

ENSEMBLE.
SAVE HIM, SAVE HIM, SAVE HIM.

CLARENCE. (*Listens, and although he'd like to oblige:*) I ... don't hear anything.

JOSEPH. Listen in your heart of hearts. Soon it will be clear.

[Music #3B: INCIDENTAL SAVE HIMS]

ENSEMBLE.
SAVE HIM!

CLARENCE. (*Thought he heard something, but—*) No...

JOSEPH. Guided by their sweet control, the prayers will help you reach your goal.

CLARENCE. (*Almost afraid to ask.*) I'll win my wings?

JOSEPH. And save his soul. Close your eyes—and hear!

(*CLARENCE covers his eyes as LIGHTS fall on him and rise on ENSEMBLE, which includes George's lovely, down-to-earth wife MARY; their daughter ZUZU, about six, who wears a robe and nightgown; MOTHER BAILEY, wise and strong; brother*

*HARRY, handsome in his Navy pilot's uniform;
UNCLE BILLY, a likable if sometimes foolish man;
GOWER, an aging druggist; BERT, a uniformed
policeman; ERNIE, a cab driver in a peaked cap; and
VI, a button-cute flirt who, in her own way, loves
George almost as much as Mary does.*
*MOTHER, ZUZU, MARY and VI are in the foreground
as the ENSEMBLE stand and kneel in various
positions of prayer before a scrim and drop which
together represent Main Street and thereby the entire
town.*
*On the scrim the trees of a parkway glisten with snow.
Buildings on the drop include a bank and the Bailey
Savings & Loan. There is also a church and, a bit
farther off, a water tower on which is painted
"BEDFORD FALLS.")*

[Music #4A: AN AMERICAN CAROL]

ENSEMBLE.
SAVE HIM! SAVE HIM! SAVE HIM! (*Etc.*)
  MOTHER.
A QUARTER TO CHRISTMAS!
  VI.
ALTHOUGH WE MIGHT—
  MARY.
HAVE ONCE COME TO CAROL:
  ZUZU.
SILENT NIGHT!
  MEN.
FRAZZLED FROM THE FESTIVE FRAY,
  WOMEN.
PREPARED TO SING TILL BREAK OF DAY—
  BERT.
NOW A FRIEND HAS LOST HIS WAY ...!
  MARY.
AND SO WE PRAY,
DEAR SAVIOUR ADORED!

ALL.
THE LITTLE TOWN OF BEDFORD FALLS
BEGS YOU SAVE HIM, LORD!
    INDIVIDUALS. (*Trailing off.*)
SAVE HIM ... SAVE HIM ... SAVE HIM ...
    SAVE HIM ... SAVE HIM ...
    CLARENCE. Save him, huh? ... Is that *my* job?
(*Discouraged.*) I wouldn't know where to start.
    JOSEPH. You've only heard what's in their souls—
Now *see* what's in their hearts.

(*LIGHTS and MUSIC up, GEORGE appears onstage
    with:*)

    ENSEMBLE. (*Delighted.*) George!!! (*THEY draw him
in as they sing:*)

                [Music #4B: SAVE GEORGE]
    HARRY.
WHO COULD SAVE THE BAILEY SAVINGS
    AND LOAN?
    MOTHER.
SAVE GEORGE!
    ENSEMBLE.
SAVE GEORGE!
    ERNIE.
WHO COULD BRAVE AN ANGRY MOB ON
    HIS OWN?
    MARY.
BUT GEORGE!
    ENSEMBLE.
OUR GEORGE!
    UNCLE BILLY.
WHEN OLD MAN POTTER PUT HIS THUMB
    IN THE PIE,
    MOTHER.
WHO STOOD UP—
    UNCLE BILLY. Ha!

MOTHER.
—AND SPAT IN HIS EYE?
BERT.
WHO THE HECK IS JUST ONE HELLUVA
GUY?
ENSEMBLE.
SAVE GEORGE! SAVE GEORGE!

(GEORGE, although shy, seems to thoroughly enjoy it as their dance about him continues—complete with "Oom-pah-pahs" and "Toodle-oos." At dance's finish:)

GOWER.
WHO SAID, "MR. GOWER, YOU MADE A
MISTAKE!"?
MOTHER.
SAVE GEORGE!
ENSEMBLE.
SAVE GEORGE!
VI.
AND SAVED ME FROM ONE I WAS TRYING
TO MAKE?
ZUZU. *(Spoken with pride.)* That's my daddy!
ENSEMBLE.
OUR GEORGE!
HARRY.
WHEN I WAS A LITTLE KID UNDER THE ICE
WHO JUMPED IN—
UNCLE BILLY. Ha!
HARRY.
—AND DIDN'T THINK TWICE?
MOTHER. *(A heartfelt prayer.)*
GIVE US YOUR STRENGTH!...
VI.
BUT TAKE OUR ADVICE!...
ENSEMBLE.
SAVE GEORGE!... SAVE GEORGE!
SAVE ... SAVE GEORGE!

(THEY finish with a flourish, LIGHTS falling on them and rising on CLARENCE.)

CLARENCE. Oh, I *like* George Bailey! And I'd like to help. But how?

JOSEPH. You'll know all you need to ... before I tell you: *"Now!"*

CLARENCE. *(Getting the cue right.)* "Now?"

JOSEPH. Now!... You see, George not only saved his little brother Harry—which cost him the hearing in his left ear...

CLARENCE. *(Doing his best to keep up with him.)* Uh ... under the ice, you mean.

JOSEPH. Still little more than a child himself, he saved yet another ... by refusing to deliver a prescription that the druggist—

CLARENCE. *(Refers to Ensemble area.)* Mr.—Gower, was it?

JOSEPH. Mr. Gower—had inadvertently poisoned.

CLARENCE. Goodness! I—I have another question. That, uh, rather striking young woman—

JOSEPH. The blonde? Violet? A very good friend of George's.

CLARENCE. I meant the dark-haired one.

JOSEPH. Mary! Who was, and still is, much more than just a friend.

CLARENCE. Mary. Hmm. *(Seems to savor the name, he likes it so much.)* How ... did George meet *her*?

JOSEPH. George *always* knew Mary.

CLARENCE. *(Amazement.)* Oh?

JOSEPH. Or so it seemed to George. He never really *met* her, however, until the night he walked her home from his brother Harry's high school prom—

CLARENCE. *(Confused.)* Harry's prom?

JOSEPH. Yes. Where George and Mary danced and— *(With a chuckle.)* swam together for the first time.

CLARENCE. *(More confused.)* Swam?

JOSEPH. The dance floor was built directly over a swimming pool, you understand (*Cuts himself off as HE realizes the difficulty of explaining all this to a more and more confused-looking CLARENCE.*) Never mind. Just watch.

(*MUSIC. CLARENCE turns his head, his SPOT dying, and Main Street comes up full. The winter scrim with its glistening trees has been replaced by a summer scrim whose trees bear leaves and blossoms. It is evening and, except for the glow of some storefront LIGHTS, the darkened drop is little more than a back-lit silhouette of buildings against the sky. We see the water tower clearly, however, its message: "BEDFORD FALLS," and a large cardboard cutout bush—set to the L. of C.*
Apparently much younger than when we first met them, GEORGE and MARY enter to the MUSIC, carrying bundles of their sodden clothing. SHE wears a terry cloth robe so large that we can't tell if she has shoes, much less anything else. HE wears the shirt and pants of an ill-fitting football uniform.)

[Music #5: SAVE GEORGE REPRISE]

MARY & GEORGE. (*Having the time of their lives.*)
OH, OH, OH ...
WHO COULD TURN A CALM NIGHT INTO A
     SQUALL?
GEORGE. (*Ready to take the blame.*)
SAVE GEORGE?
MARY. (*Agrees.*)
SAVE GEORGE!
GEORGE. (*Mimes a slide trombone.*)
DA DAH DAH ...
MARY. (*A happier question.*)
WHO COULD TURN A PROM NIGHT INTO A
     BALL?

GEORGE. (*Glad to take the credit.*)
SAVE GEORGE?
MARY. (*Agrees.*)
SAVE GEORGE!
GEORGE.
DA DAH DAH ...
MARY.
WHO WOULD TRY THE CHARLESTON JUST
ON A WHIM?
TILL THEY SPLIT—
GEORGE. Ha!
MARY.
THE FLOOR IN THE GYM?
GEORGE.
WHO WAS AWFUL GLAD ... HE KNEW HOW
TO SWIM?
MARY. (*Spoken.*) Save Mary?
GEORGE. Save—
Together. (*In close and varying harmony.*)
GEORGE...!

GEORGE. (*Buttons it.*) Hot dog. (*THEY have finished their dance, arms out-stretched, MARY sitting on his knee. HE turns to her and, after a pause, shy but meaningful.*) Hey, Mary...

MARY. (*As aware of their proximity as he is.*) Oh oh.

GEORGE. (*Mildly chastises as SHE starts away.*) Now don't. Don't walk away like that.

MARY. (*Turns to him, an honest, open-eyed question.*) ... Why?

GEORGE. *Why?*

MARY. (*Quietly, as open-eyed as ever.*) ... Why?

GEORGE. (*Thinking fast.*) Because—don't cha see?, I—I might follow you, and ... (*Notices her trailing terry cloth belt, which now lies still at her feet.*) Maybe step on your belt ... I do tend to be a clumsy lout ...

MARY. (*Also notices the belt, interested.*) Oh?

GEORGE. That big white robe of yours'd—zzzt!—come right off ...

MARY. (*Startled—yet more and more interested.*) Oh?

GEORGE. And although fortunately—or *un*fortunately, depending on your point of view, I guess—my back would probably be turned at the time ...

MARY. (*Seems disappointed.*) Oh.

GEORGE. (*To the rescue.*) Still ... you'd have to hide...

MARY. (*Excited again, looks about.*) Where?

GEORGE. (*Inspired, points.*) ... In that old hydrangea bush!

MARY. Uh *huh.*

GEORGE. (*His point.*) And that would create ... a Very Interesting Situation.

MARY. (*Considers, aware how close he is to her.*) Then ... you're suggesting I ... (*Voice ready to break.*) *don't* walk away—?

GEORGE. (*Close, almost touching,* his *voice ready to break.*) I don't think ... we could stand the scandal. (*Attempts to kiss her but:*)

MARY. (*Starts to laugh.*) Oh!

GEORGE. (*Startled, he is so caught up in her.*) Huh?

MARY. (*Half-laughing, half-complaining.*) George! That kind of thing—hiding in a bush, for heaven's sake don't you know it only happens in the movies?

GEORGE. (*Didn't quite catch it, cups his good right ear.*) In the what?

MARY. The movies.

GEORGE. (*Simultaneously.*) Oh, the movies, yeah.

MARY. (*Now not so sure.*) ... I *think* so.

GEORGE. (*After a painful pause, recovers.*) OK—then I'll throw a rock at the old Granville house.

MARY. (*"Sees" the house over heads of audience, fondly.*) Don't! Please don't! I love that old house.

GEORGE. (*Can't believe it.*) That run-down, deserted, old relic?

MARY. Really, there is something so romantic—(*But sees HE is preparing to throw.*) Oh don't.

GEORGE. (*Simultaneous with this last.*) The object is to break some glass, y'see ... (*Hurls a "rock"—and we hear the satisfying SHATTER OF GLASS. Pleased:*) *Hot* dog, I guess I get my wish.

MARY. (*Disappointed in him.*) ... Which was?

GEORGE. Didn't Harry tell you? Now that he's taking my place at the Savings and Loan—I mean, I worked for my dad for *four years* just waiting for this ...

MARY. (*A sigh of realization.*) Oh yes. You're leaving in the morning to "see the world." (*Half-angry, disappointed, would move away from him, but HE takes her arms so intensely that HE is almost rough with her. Doesn't she understand?*)

GEORGE. No no, Mary. Not just to *see* it ... (*Reacts as we hear the plaintive—and, to him, torturing—WHISTLE of a far-off train. Then:*) I—I've been *seeing* it night and day—in my dreams, in my National Geographics—ever since I was a kid. Now—I want to *hear* it too. (*Another WHISTLE. HE reacts even more sharply and, with a groan from his soul.*) Oh Mary. I gotta get out of this town.

[Music #6: SEE AND HEAR THE WORLD]

(*Sings.*)
EVERY TIME I HEAR A PASSING TRAIN,
    MARY!—
I GET FEELINGS THAT I CAN'T EXPLAIN,
    MARY!
GOTTA GET OUT! GOTTA! SEE AND HEAR
    THE WORLD!
THE BANKS OF THE SEINE, A THUNDERING
    PLANE!
THE RATTLE OF AN ... ANCHOR CHAIN!

I GOTTA SNAP THE STRINGS OF THIS OLD
    TOWN, MARY!

GOTTA GO BEFORE THEY TIE ME DOWN,
    MARY!
GOTTA GET OUT! GONNA! ONLY GOT ONE
    SHOT!
AND I GOTTA, GOTTA SEE AND HEAR THE
    WORLD!
    (*Speaks over VAMP.*)
Then college—where they can impart
The knowledge—to give me a start
Perfecting—an architect's plan ...
Erecting—a city that's new ...
Connecting—a mile-long span ...
Projecting—an airfield too!
    (*Sings.*)
I WILL BUILD A SHINING TOWER IN THE
    SKY...
AND THEN I'LL BUILD ONE REALLY...
    REALLY...

(*As HE seems to "strain," MUSIC STOPS and HE points
    to MARY, who takes and holds the note in the highest
    octave she can handle.*)

    MARY.
HIGH!...
    GEORGE. (*Over rising crescendo as SHE holds note.*)
I'LL BUILD AND BUILD AND BUILD AND
    BUILD
AND BUILD AND BUILD AND BUILD! ...

(*Again the WHISTLE. BOTH stop. Then:*)

WHEN I HEAR THE WHISTLE OF A TRAIN,
    MARY!—
IT CAN MAKE ME ALMOST GO INSANE,
    MARY!
GOTTA GET OUT! GOTTA! SEE AND HEAR
    THE WORLD!

AN INDIAN RAJ, A JAPANESE OWL!
THE RAIN UPON THE ... TAJ MAHAL!

I GOTTA SHAKE THE MUD OF THIS OLD
   TOWN, MARY!
GOTTA GO OR I JUST KNOW I'LL DROWN,
   MARY!
GOTTA GET OUT! GONNA! EVERY FLAG
   UNFURLED!
THE WORLD'S A SONG I—VOW T' HEAR!
THE BREAK OF DAWN I'M—OUTA HERE!
I GOTTA—SEE AND HEAR THE WORLD!

*(When HE is finished, MARY calmly picks up a "rock"
and, although her bathrobe makes the action awkward,
throws the rock toward the Granville house. There is
no sound whatsoever. GEORGE tries to explain.)*

GEORGE. You're supposed to *break* something ...
(*And now—a SHATTER that's louder and longer than
George's was.*)
MARY. (*Quietly smug.*) *Hot* dog. (*Starts away.*)
GEORGE. Hey! Did you make a wish too? Mary? What
did you wish for? Mary! Wait!

*(SHE exits L., GEORGE in pursuit—and VI, who, like
MARY, wears an all-encompassing bathrobe, steps out
from behind the bush.)*

VI. (*Removes a couple of leaves from her hair as SHE
looks after them.*) Wow. *That* was close. (*Crosses length
of stage to R. Stops and turns just before exiting to call.*)
Are you coming, Sam?

(BLACKOUT. LIGHTS rise on CLARENCE.)

CLARENCE. (*Curiosity compelling him.*) Maybe I
should have asked how George met *her*.

JOSEPH. (*Surprised at him.*) Clarence!

CLARENCE. (*Hurries to ask.*) He—he *did* marry one of them, didn't he?

JOSEPH. (*Assures him.*) We'll get to that.

CLARENCE. (*Persists.*) Will we get to what Mary *wished* for?

JOSEPH. ... Soon.

CLARENCE. (*Would demand.*) At least tell me this much—*now,* can you? *Did* George see the world? Did he *hear* it?

JOSEPH. As it happened ... his father died that very night—

CLARENCE. (*Startled.*) *Oh.*

JOSEPH. —and George was asked to forget his trip, forget going off to school, and to take over the Savings and Loan.

CLARENCE. But he couldn't! Could he? Not give up his plans!?...

JOSEPH. Either that or lose the business his father had founded—to Potter.

CLARENCE. (*Seems to remember.*) Potter?!... I've *heard* that name.

JOSEPH. (*Sadly.*) Not up here, I'm afraid.

CLARENCE. (*Shocked.*) No?

JOSEPH. (*Would explain.*) The richest and meanest man in the county. A frustrated, miserable man.

(*BLACKOUT on CLARENCE. LIGHTS up in the Savings & Loan's outer office, which consists of little more than a desk so small that it's really a work table. The scrim and drop are dark as GEORGE, now wearing a business suit with a black band on the sleeve, confronts POTTER, an aging bull of a man who sits in a throne-like wheel chair. UNCLE BILLY, who sits at his desk in shirt sleeves in a wheeled swivel chair, pores over reports as VI stands at his side in a skirt and blouse, her sleeves pushed up like a*

*working girl. BOTH pretend to be unaware of the
confrontation between GEORGE and POTTER.)*

GEORGE. (*Angry.*) And another thing, Mr. Potter—!
POTTER. (*Quite as angry, but more controlled.*) Now
now, George—you just go back in there ...
GEORGE. Listen!
POTTER. (*Overrides him.*) Go back and talk to that
Board of Directors the way you've just talked to me!
We'll *see* if the Bailey Savings and Loan survives!
GEORGE. It'll survive, Mr. Potter. It'll be here when
you're dead and gone!
POTTER. Ha! (*But GEORGE is already exiting L. in
the direction Potter pointed. The tall, sepulchral
POTTER'S MAN—who seems more mortician than
valet—enters to wheel POTTER off R.*) Bailey ... Bailey
... I am sick of *Bailey!* First there's Peter! Now there's
George! I *hate* the Bailey name!

*(Only when POTTER and POTTER'S MAN exit does
UNCLE BILLY dare turn to Vi.)*

UNCLE BILLY. (*Softly.*) Did you hear, Violet? Did you
listen to the meeting?
VI. (*Deliciously.*) I heard, Uncle Billy! Oh, that Potter
took a beating! (*HARRY, also in shirt sleeves, enters
from up right. SHE addresses him, a little louder.*) Did
you hear, Harry Bailey—what your brother told the
board?
HARRY. (*Quite as delicious.*) I heard what he told
Potter—every loving word!

(BERT, GOWER, and ERNIE enter from L.)

[Music #7A: A FRUSTRATED MAN]

BERT.
I WAS UNDERNEATH THE CLOCK!

GOWER.
I WAS JUST ABOUT TO LOCK!
ERNIE.
I WAS HALFWAY DOWN THE BLOCK!
BERT, GOWER & ERNIE. (*In harmony.*)
AND WE HEARD!...
UNCLE BILLY. (*Laughs, clicks his heels, he feels so good.*)
OH! DID GEORGE EVER TELL HIM!
BERT. Sure did!
UNCLE BILLY.
OH! DID GEORGE SHOW HIS STUFF!
VI. Some stuff!
UNCLE BILLY.
TAKING NONE OF HIS GUFF,
HE CALLED OLD POTTER'S BLUFF.
TILL POTTER SPUTTERED AND MUTTERED,
  "ENOUGH!"...

(*MOTHER enters from L., wearing black, addresses Uncle Billy.*)

MOTHER. (*Fearing the worst.*)
DID THE MEETING GO SMOOTHLY?
UNCLE BILLY. (*Speaks, feigning dejection.*) No, it went rough. (*Takes his swivel chair and swings it D.S., all the while singing, reassuring, strong:*)
... UNTIL GEORGE TURNED TO POTTER
  AND SAID...
THE OTHERS.
YES, HE SAID!...
UNCLE BILLY. (*In one—continued—neat motion, turns chair to face him, addresses it.*)
YOU'RE A FRUSTRATED MAN, HENRY
  POTTER!
THE OTHERS. (*Also address chair.*)
YOU ARE!

UNCLE BILLY.
YOU'RE A FRUSTRATED, HATED OLD
   SCUM!
THE OTHERS.
OLD SCUM!
   UNCLE BILLY.
YOU'RE AS SLY AS A SNAKE!
   ERNIE.
ON THE MAKE!
   BERT.
ON THE TAKE!
   GOWER.
YOU'RE A MUGGER!
   VI.
A BUGGER!
   UNCLE BILLY.
A BUM!
   THE OTHERS.
WHAT A BUM!
   UNCLE BILLY. (*With relish as HE and OTHERS begin
to move the chair all over the stage.*)
YOU'RE A FRUSTRATED MAN, HENRY
   POTTER!
   VI. (*To Mother.*) George said it!
   UNCLE BILLY.
YOU'RE A FRUSTRATED, DATED OLD
   CRUMB!
   GOWER. (*To Mother.*) We all heard!
   UNCLE BILLY.
YOU'RE AN ACHE IN THE BUTT!
   ERNIE.
YOU'RE A FAKE!
   BERT.
YOU'RE A NUT!
   GOWER.
YOU'RE A CROOK!
   VI.
YOU'RE A SCHNOOK!

UNCLE BILLY.
AND YOU'RE DUMB!
    THE OTHERS.
DUMB!... DUMB!... DUMB!
    MOTHER. (*Almost in shock through all this.*) But why—
    UNCLE BILLY. (*To chair.*)
TO THINK YOU'D ACTUALLY KNOCK MY
    FATHER!
    MOTHER. (*In greater shock, getting angry.*) Potter did that?
    UNCLE BILLY. (*As VI nods to Mother.*)
WHO'S TWICE THE MAN YOU ARE, GEORGE
    SAID!
    BERT.
EVEN DEAD!

(*ALL look at Bert before:*)

    UNCLE BILLY. (*Agrees.*) Right! (*Sings.*)
OK, I DON'T KNOW WHY HE'D BOTHER TO
    TRY,
WITH ALL THE MANY SHANTIES YOU RENT
    AND OWN,
TO BUILD THIS PENNY ANTE SAVINGS AND
    LOAN!

NOT A MAN OF BUSINESS BUT A MAN OF
    HEART,
HE KNEW ONE THING WAS NEEDED FROM
    THE START...
    HARRY. Ma, you'd've been so proud of George when he said—(*To the chair.*) Don't you know, Mr. Potter, what the people, the little people, the people who do most of the living and dying around here—Don't you know what they *want*?
    UNCLE BILLY. (*Quietly assures him.*) Take it.

[Music #7B: FOUR WALLS AND A CEILING]

HARRY. (*A pure, clear voice.*)
FOUR WALLS AND A CEILING—
MOTHER. (*To Harry, touched.*) Oh, your father loved
that song!
HARRY.
A YARD FULL OF FLOWERS.
FOUR WALLS AND A CEILING—
THAT WE CAN CALL OURS!
(*Pauses, uncertain.*) Then, uh...
MOTHER. (*Helps.*)
NO BALUSTRADE BALLROOMS—
HARRY. That's it!
MOTHER.
NO TOWERS OR THRONE.
SOME LARGE AND SOME SMALL ROOMS ...
ONE ALL FOR OUR OWN.
HARRY. (*Grins.*) You and Dad, huh?
ALL. (*As UNCLE BILLY gestures to them.*)
FOUR WALLS AND A CEILING ...
MOTHER.
NO MIGHTY EXPANSE ...
ALL.
FOUR WALLS AND A CEILING ...
HARRY.
AND WE'LL HAVE OUR CHANCE!...
MOTHER. (*Laughs.*) You remember!
HARRY AND MOTHER.
IT'S JUST SO APPEALING!
WE'RE SURE TO SUCCEED!
ALL.
FOUR WALLS AND A CEILING ...
IS ALL WE NEED.

(*HARRY bows to his Mother, inviting her to dance.*)

MOTHER. Oh, I haven't done this in years!

(THEY dance.)

THE OTHERS. (*Come in with.*)
FOUR WALLS AND A CEILING—
THAT WE CAN CALL OURS!...
  HARRY AND MOTHER.
IT'S JUST SO APPEALING!
WE'RE SURE TO SUCCEED!
  ALL.
FOUR WALLS AND A CEILING ...
IS ALL WE NEED.

(THEY finish and HARRY kisses his Mother.)

UNCLE BILLY. Hey, that's great! You and Harry were just—(*Stops as GEORGE reenters with an envelope for Harry.*)
GEORGE. (*Angry—to cover his loss.*) Harry!... You still want to go to college? (*HARRY, lost, turns to his Mother. GEORGE addresses her, the loss showing through.*) The board ... voted. They said they'd kill the Savings and Loan ... until I told 'em I'd stay here and run it.
MOTHER. (*Immediately sensitive to his plight, reaches out to touch him.*) Oh George—! (*LIGHTS drop in office, up on CLARENCE.*)
CLARENCE. (*In sympathy.*) Oh nuts! He *did* stay.
JOSEPH. (*Sighs.*) ... Yes. Having given the tuition money he'd saved to Harry—
CLARENCE. (*Throws up his hands, knows George by now.*) What else???
JOSEPH. —George started saving again. The plan was, Harry would take over when he returned with his degree. But ... Harry never quite returned.
CLARENCE. (*Prepared for the worst.*) ... No?

JOSEPH. (*Reassures him.*) He married a wonderful girl, Clarence, and took a research job—something he was very good at—in a city far away.

CLARENCE. (*Sour.*) The best-laid plans, eh?... (*Shakes his head.*) I wonder why that is. I've been up here two hundred years and nobody's *yet* explained to me why that is!

JOSEPH. George, of course, urged him to take the job.

CLARENCE. (*Glum, ironic.*) An honorable man.

JOSEPH. (*Adds to Clarence's thought.*)—who had learned long before that being honorable and being miserable are *not* mutually exclusive.

CLARENCE. Nobody's explained *that* to me either. (*Pause.*) When did he finally kiss her?

JOSEPH. Who?

CLARENCE. Mary—Violet—one of 'em.

JOSEPH. Not till the night of the wedding.

CLARENCE. (*Confused.*) Whose wedding? *Harry's?*

JOSEPH. Harry's.

[Music #8A: WEDDINGS AND WHISKEY GLASSES]

(*MUSIC: The first seven notes of the closing phrase of the Lohengrin Wedding March—as LIGHTS fall on CLARENCE and rise on George's back yard.*

It's summer again, night again, but the storefronts are completely dark, only the "BEDFORD FALLS" tower apparent. Clearly, we are witnessing the aftermath of a celebration. We see a bench, two chairs, and a white picket fence—which, we'll discover, consists of two lengths abutting—and a table on which there are several glasses lined up, each with a different amount of what seems to be whiskey.

GEORGE, BERT, and ERNIE, all wearing suits, ties open, lounge about in various stages of letdown— more tired than intoxicated. VIOLET, wearing a pretty party dress, sits to one side, her eyes on George. Only UNCLE BILLY seems to be fully enjoying the moment as HE stands behind the glasses, using a spoon to CLINK out [picking immediately up from the MUSIC we've just heard] the March's eighth through fifteenth notes on five of the glasses, each supplying a different pitch.

HE pauses after hitting the final note—which happens to be the only sour one—picks up the first glass he struck [not the last], mimes sipping a bit from it and strikes it again—the note ringing true and pleasing him immensely.)

UNCLE BILLY. Ahhh!

(General applause and huzzahs.)

ERNIE. Not bad, Uncle Billy.

GEORGE. (*Approving.*) You could take an act like that on the road—if you could bottle it.

BERT. I thought it *came* in bottles. (*Takes one of Uncle Billy's glasses and drinks from it.*)

UNCLE BILLY. (*Incensed.*) Say—!

GEORGE. (*The peacemaker.*) Now now, there's plenty where that came from ...

VI. (*As GEORGE looks about, trying to find a bottle.*) It's in the house. I'll find it, Georgie. (*What she says is not as important as the sultry, languid, and knowing way she says it. Nor is the way she says it as important as the way she walks, hips moving under her summer dress as SHE heads for the right—and the house—the three younger men taking notice.*)

BERT. I'll—help her find it. (*Starts after her.*)

ERNIE. (*Already moving.*) I'll help him help her. (*Follows the two out as GEORGE grins, shaking his head, and then, remembering where the extra bottle is, reaches into Uncle Billy's inside coat pocket, takes it out and hands it to him.*)

GEORGE. Here you are, sir.

UNCLE BILLY. What? (*After studying bottle doubtfully.*) ... I'll try it. (*Takes a swig and resumes his work as HARRY enters from L., also wearing a suit, but looking sharp and young and handsome—as HARRY always does.*)

HARRY. Say, fellas, I just wanted to thank you for— (*Looks about.*) Where'd everybody go?

GEORGE. (*The philosopher.*) The way of all flesh, I'm sorry to say.

HARRY. (*Puzzled.*) Oh?... (*Then.*) George, mostly I wanted to thank *you*.

GEORGE. (*Doesn't want to hear it.*) Now, now...

HARRY. If you hadn't given us your blessing, I don't know what—

GEORGE. (*So uncomfortable HE's almost angry.*) Well, of course you have my blessing. For Pete's sake, Harry.

WOMAN'S VOICE. (*Off, sweet and—without trying to be—sexy.*) Harry!

GEORGE. (*Looks L. toward the sound of the voice, more in control, big brotherly.*) Just, uh ... do a lot of good research, will you?

HARRY. (*Promises.*) I will!

WOMAN'S VOICE. (*Calls again, doesn't know where he is.*) The train won't wait, Harry! Are you out there?

HARRY. (*Ready to go.*) Be right with you, hon!

GEORGE. (*Still looks toward the sound of the voice.*) And if it should result in any new products ...

HARRY. (*Doesn't get it.*) Hmmm?

GEORGE. (*Quietly.*) See that you name one after me.

HARRY. (*Gets it, grins.*) I will! I will, George! (*Shakes George's hand vigorously.*) Good bye, Uncle Billy! (*Exits L.*)

UNCLE BILLY. (*Who throughout has been "experimentally" pouring from the bottle George gave him, shaking his head, sipping some, and pouring again—now looks up.*) Mmmmm? (*To George.*) Is Harry gone?

GEORGE. Just this second, yeah.

UNCLE BILLY. (*Waves and calls without looking.*) Good bye, Harry! (*Comes to his feet.*) Seems to me, when I started, I was using a better grade of whiskey. (*Explains, confidential.*) Truer in tone.

GEORGE. I'm sure.

UNCLE BILLY. I believe—there's more in the house.

GEORGE. So everybody says ...

UNCLE BILLY. (*Momentarily befuddled.*) Which way's the house?

GEORGE. (*Shows him by turning his shoulders.*) That way.

UNCLE BILLY. (*Having second thoughts, takes the bottle George gave him, explains.*) Just in case I don't find it.

GEORGE. (*Can't resist.*) The whiskey or the house?

UNCLE BILLY. Yes! (*Exits R. unsteadily, sings.*)
MY WILD IRISH ROSE ...

(*There is a CRASH as of garbage cans.*)

UNCLE BILLY. I'm all *right*! I'm all *right*!...
(*Continues singing, voice trailing off.*)
THE SWEETEST FLOWER THAT GROWS...

[Music #8B: SEE THE WORLD INCIDENTAL]

(*MUSIC: A few plaintive notes from "See and Hear the World" as GEORGE, who is alone now, removes travel folders from his jacket and examines them, perhaps thinking of what might have been. As MUSIC ends, a TRAIN WHISTLE is heard. HE looks toward the sound, hurting, puts the folders away, and is joined by MOTHER, who enters from R.*)

MOTHER. (*All too aware of what is going on inside him, gives him a quick kiss on the lips.*) That's for nothin'.

GEORGE. (*More warm with her than uncomfortable, knowing she is simply showing motherly concern.*) Hmmm. (*Another CRASH from R. As BOTH look:*)

UNCLE BILLY. (*Protests.*) I'm all *right!*

MOTHER. I'd ask what got into *him*—but I imagine that's a silly question.

GEORGE. (*Nods.*) I imagine.

MOTHER. (*Delicately.*) Did you know ... Mary Hatch is back from college?

GEORGE. (*Not interested.*) Did you know... it's the third time you mentioned it?

MOTHER. (*In all sincerity.*) She could help you find the answer, George.

GEORGE. (*With a glance toward the house.*) So could Violet Bick.

MOTHER. (*Shocked.*) Violet Bick?

GEORGE. Depending, of course—on what the question is.

MOTHER. (*Insists.*) Can you give me one good reason you shouldn't see Mary?

GEORGE. Sure. Sam Wainwright.

MOTHER. Old "Hee Haw"?

GEORGE. (*Cups right ear, not having quite heard her.*) Hmmm? (*Then, realizes.*) Old "Hee Haw," yeah. He's crazy about her.

MOTHER. She isn't so crazy about *him.* Why, she lights up like a firefly whenever you're around. Besides—she's in Bedford Falls, Sam's in New York.

GEORGE. Where *I* should probably be, ha?

MOTHER. (*Protests.*) No!

GEORGE. (*Turns on her, at last expressing the anger that has been boiling up within him for years.*) Oh, Mother, you—you come out here with your games! Don't you know I've played these games with Potter every day for the last four years? "Do this, do that, help yourself out, George—or let *me* help you, son!" Don't you know I'm *tired* of being manipulated? (*TRAIN WHISTLE. HE looks toward it, bitter.*) That's my train—and it's left the station. (*Moves D.S., as determined as HE is angry.*) Get this straight, Ma—I *won't* be getting married! Not to anybody! Not ever! And if I do—it won't be Mary Hatch!

[Music #9: IF YOU'D ONLY SEE HER]

MOTHER. But ... (*Hurting for him, moves down to him, as there is MUSIC and a subtle change in the LIGHT, the scrim and drop fading to black as a new, dream-like color is cast on the scene. Sings.*)
GEORGE! GEORGE! IF YOU'D ONLY SEE
    HER!
GEORGE! GEORGE! IF YOU'D ONLY GO!
GEORGE! GEORGE! WHAT YOU NEED CAN
    BE HER!
YOU'LL LOVE HER SO!
OH, DON'T YOU (KNOW?) ...

(*VI enters from L., a hand out to him.*)

VI.
(KNOW,) GEORGE, THOUGH I LIKE YOU
    VERY
MUCH, GEORGE, AND I'VE HAD MY FUN—
(*As HE goes to her.*)
TOUCH, GEORGE—
(*Touches and turns him.*)
THEN GO BE WITH MARY!
SHE IS THE ONE! THE (ONE!)

(*HARRY and GOWER enter from L., UNCLE BILLY, BERT and ERNIE from R.*)

THE MEN.
(WON)DER AS TO WHY, GEORGE, ALL THE
    PLANS YOU'VE PLANNED ON
DIE, GEORGE, AS THEY'VE DIED?

THE WOMEN.
YOU MUST NOT CRY, GEORGE, BUT WITH
    ALL ABANDON,
FLY, GEORGE, TO HER SIDE!...

(So singing, THEY separate the fence into halves, swinging them around to create a kind of "funnel" or tapering pathway—in the center of which MARY stands, radiant.)

MARY.
GEORGE! GEORGE! I'VE BEEN DREAMING
    OF YOU
FROM, GEORGE, SINCE WE'VE FIRST
    BEGUN!
COME, GEORGE, YOU MUST KNOW I LOVE
    YOU!
WE CAN BE TWO IN (ONE!)

(GEORGE and MARY come together, hands touching, and move D.S., eyes only for each other, MARY calm and assuring, GEORGE caught up in her spell, but still not at all sure this is a good thing.)

THE OTHERS.
(WON)DER AS TO WHY, GEORGE, ALL THE
    PLANS YOU'VE PLANNED ON
DIE, GEORGE, AS THEY'VE DIED?
YOU MUST NOT CRY, GEORGE, BUT WITH
    ALL ABANDON,
FLY, GEORGE, TO HER SIDE!...

(LIGHTS drop on all but GEORGE and MARY.)

GEORGE. *(Tortured, speaks more than sings.)*
Mary!... I've been dreaming of you!
Mary!... Since we've first begun!

Mary!... Must I say... I love you?... (*Breaks off stupidly.*) Oh, Mary! Mary!

(*No longer able to stop himself, embraces her almost savagely. MUSIC up, the LIGHTS fall as THEY kiss and cling to each other.*
After a moment, LIGHTS rise on CLARENCE—as HE noisily BLOWS his nose. Turns to Joseph.)

CLARENCE. (*At peace.*) Y'know? I kinda *hoped* it'd be her. Almost said a little prayer.

JOSEPH. His mother said a *lot* of them, believe me.

CLARENCE. (*Quickly, lest Joseph think he is lacking in faith.*) Oh, I do! (*Sound of RAIN pouring. Curious.*) ... What's that?

JOSEPH. Their wedding day, Clarence. Their wedding day and the rain.

CLARENCE. (*Fearful at this apparent omen.*) Oh oh.

JOSEPH. (*Would assure him.*) It wasn't so bad. Really. They had a fine ceremony, a wonderful reception...

CLARENCE. (*Suspicious.*) Go on.

JOSEPH. Well, they planned to see New York City and maybe a little part of Europe on their honeymoon ...

CLARENCE. (*More suspicious.*) Go on.

JOSEPH. (*Uncomfortable.*) In fact, Ernie, the cab driver, was just taking them to the train station when, uh...

CLARENCE. (*Even more suspicious.*) Yes—?

JOSEPH. Well, times were hard ...

CLARENCE. And?

JOSEPH. (*"Caught," sighs.*) They witnessed a run on the Savings and Loan.

CLARENCE. (*Not that familiar with the term.*) A run???

JOSEPH. Folks wanted their savings and wanted them *now*—even though *no* institution ever has all that cash on hand. Mary, of course, warned him not to stop, but George—

CLARENCE. (*Ahead of him.*) Oh, I know.
JOSEPH. (*Without pause.*)—well, he *had* to see what
he could do to help.
CLARENCE. (*Nods, fatalistic.*) That's George.
JOSEPH. (*Sticks up for George.*) It was *important.*
Potter had warned him that if the day ever came he
couldn't make good on a debt, the Savings and Loan
would be finished.
CLARENCE. (*Thinking about it.*) Oh? (*Thinks some
more about it.*) Oh.

(*LIGHTS down on CLARENCE and up on the S&L
outer office where UNCLE BILLY sits alone at his
desk. RAIN sound gives way to INTRODUCTORY
MUSIC and:*)

[Music #10: MONEY]

VARIOUS INDIVIDUALS. (*Off, overlapping, like moans
from hell.*) Money!... Money!... Money!... Money!...
Money!... Money!... Money!... Money!... Money!...
Money!... Money!... Money!...

(*And now THEY enter from all sides—hidden from the
audience by the large black umbrellas THEY carry and
thoroughly frightening UNCLE BILLY as THEY sing
in slow and threatening anger.*)

THE CROWD.
MONEY!
MONEY!...
WHERE'S OUR MONEY?...

MONEY!
MONEY!...
WHERE'S OUR MONEY?...

MONEY!

MONEY!...
WHERE'S OUR MONEY?...

WE WANT OUR MONEY NOW!

(THEY have just closed in on UNCLE BILLY when GEORGE enters in a raincoat, wet from the rain.)

GEORGE. *(Hurrying to Uncle Billy's defense, sings, driving them back.)*
NOW WAIT!...
YOU AGREED YOU WOULD ONLY
    LIQUIDATE
IF YOU GAVE US THE TIME TO GENERATE
ALL THE FUNDS THAT YOU NEED TO ON
    THE DATE
WE ASSIGNED AND AGREED TO.

THOUGH I HATE
TO DENY YOU AND PLEAD YOU HESITATE
IT IS STILL GUARANTEED YOU SURE AS
    FATE
AND INDEED YOU'LL SUCCEED TOO
IF YOU'LL WAIT, WAIT, WAIT!

I HATE
TO DENY YOU AND PLEAD YOU HESITATE,
BUT IT'S STILL GUARANTEED YOU SURE
    AS FATE
AND INDEED YOU'LL SUCCEED TOO
IF YOU'LL WAIT, WAIT, WAIT!

(CROWD repeats its song with vigor as GEORGE responds in counterpoint, the tempo increasing. THEY press in on him and HE, like a dancing boxer, both avoids them and stays in the fight, occasionally daring to press back. UNCLE BILLY, who seeks to avoid the crowd altogether, can't quite get clear and has a

miserable time as HE is turned about, always in someone's way.)

(The following is sung in counterpoint:)

CROWD.	GEORGE.
MONEY!	HEY, WAIT!
MONEY!...	FOR YOU MUST
	KNOW WE
	APPRECIATE
WHERE'S OUR	THE DISTRUST
MONEY?...	THAT DIRECTS
	YOU
	DEMONSTRATE
MONEY!	YOU WILL NOT
MONEY!...	BE DISBANDED
	TILL YOU'VE
	GOT
WHERE'S OUR	EVERY CENT
MONEY?...	YOU'VE
	DEMANDED.
MONEY!	TO PRO-RATE
MONEY!...	YOUR
	EXACTIONS A
	FRACTION
WHERE'S OUR	LETS US TREAT
MONEY?...	THE ENTIRE
	TRANSACTION
MONEY!...	AS TO MEET
MONEY!...	YOUR
	COMPLETE
	SATISFACTION
WE WON'T WAIT!	IF YOU'LL WAIT,
	WAIT, WAIT!
MONEY!	PRO-RATE

MONEY!...   YOUR
                         EXACTIONS A
                         FRACTION
WHERE'S OUR   AND WE'LL
    MONEY?...   TREAT THE
                         ENTIRE
                         TRANSACTION
MONEY!   AS TO MEET
    MONEY!...   YOUR
                         COMPLETE
                         SATISFACTION
WE WON'T WAIT!   IF YOU'LL WAIT,
                         WAIT, WAIT!

*(THEY crowd in again, their grasping hands protruding
from the sides and tops of their umbrellas, forcing
GEORGE to conclude his song from the top of the
desk.)*

CROWD.   GEORGE.
MONEY!   PLEASE WAIT!
MONEY!...   THOUGH I CEDE
                           YOU THE RIGHT
                         TO
                         REMONSTRATE,
WHERE'S OUR   THE IMMEDIATE
    MONEY?...   NEED TO
                         ALLOCATE
MONEY!   ALL YOUR
    MONEY!...   FUNDS WILL
                         UNDULY
WHERE'S OUR   OBVIATE OUR
    MONEY?...   REBATING
                         THEM FULLY.

MONEY!   AND TO FILL

MONEY!...

WHERE'S OUR
   MONEY?...

MONEY!
   MONEY!...

WE WON'T WAIT,
WHERE'S OUR
   MONEY,
   GEORGE!

WE WON'T WAIT,
WHERE'S OUR
   MONEY,
   GEORGE!

THE WITH-
   DRAWALS
   REQUESTED
IS TO KILL ALL
   THE EGGS
   THAT YOU'VE
   NESTED.
SO UNTIL YOUR
   REQUESTS
   CAN BE
   VESTED,
WON'T YOU
   WAIT?

CAN'T YOU
   WAIT?

JUST WAIT!

(GEORGE and CROWD break off their song as MARY, who also wears a raincoat and has entered during this last, is suddenly in the midst of them, a sheaf of bills raised high.)

MARY. Did someone mention *money?*

(The hands withdraw.)

GEORGE. (*Not sure this is a good idea.*) Our honeymoon money???

(SHE nods. HE nods. Only then, in lowering the sheaf of bills, does SHE offer it to the CROWD, their hands immediately out and towards her. MUSIC is buttoned. LIGHTS out and up on CLARENCE.)

CLARENCE. *(Fearful.)* Was it really? Their *honeymoon* money?

JOSEPH. *(Sighs.)* It was. Not enough, of course, to pay the shareholders in full ... but George finally convinced them—most of them—to take only what they needed for now. And folks do need things, Clarence ...

CLARENCE. Oh I know.

JOSEPH. The bank had already shut down and they had bills to pay.

CLARENCE. I remember ... paying bills. *(Shudders audibly, just as glad to be out of it.)*

JOSEPH. Between the honeymoon money and some fast footwork by George, the Savings and Loan weathered the storm and the shareholders did not lose a cent.

CLARENCE. *(Wants to know.)* But George and Mary...?

JOSEPH. *(With warm assurance.)* No ... they didn't lose their honeymoon either. Mary made sure of that. While George finished up at the Savings and Loan, she managed to commandeer—

CLARENCE. *(Startled, enjoying this.)* She what???

JOSEPH. *(Without pause.)* —the old Granville house. Yes, she did. And with the help of a couple of friends ...

CLARENCE. *(Still enjoying, laughing.)* The rundown relic???

JOSEPH. Yes!... she began the job it would take her years to complete ... starting with a few discreetly placed posters.

(LIGHTS fall on CLARENCE, MUSIC beginning as MARY, beautiful in a negligee and robe, strikes a match and lights the first of two tall candles—her

*action causing LIGHTS to come up in the Granville
house. We are in the dining room, as defined by travel
posters of Paris, Cairo, London, etc. which have been
glued to long, pull-down window shades, the shades
supported by a hinged three-part frame which suggests
a shallow, glass-free bay window area and hangs some
distance in from the still darkened "Main Street." A
table has been set for two with china, a linen cloth,
wine, a covered entreé, and, of course, the candles.*
GEORGE, *mussed, tired, and still wet from the rain,
enters from U.L.*
[Music #11: INTRO: THREE WALLS AND A
CEILING]
MARY, *having lit the second candle, sees him and
watches as* HE, *curious but game, bends back part of
the left shade to peek behind it at Main Street—which
is LIGHTED simultaneous with his action...)*

GEORGE. (*Non-committal.*) Hmmm. (*... and drops to
darkness as HE releases the shade. HE wanders to the
right shade, bends it back briefly and Main Street is
LIGHTED again. Again, non-committal.*) Hmmm.
(*Releases right shade, Main Street LIGHTS dropping,
takes off his coat and turns to her—as SHE waits in all
expectancy, so hoping he'll be pleased!*)
MARY. Well? ...

[MUSIC #12: THREE WALLS AND A CEILING]

GEORGE. (*Sings.*)
THREE WALLS AND A CEILING—
MARY. (*Resists laughter.*) Oh George!
GEORGE.
SOME ACHES—
(*Indicates the glass-free windows.*)
BUT NO PANES.
MARY. (*Groans at the pun.*) Now, George—!

GEORGE.
THREE WALLS AND A CEILING—
(A "drop" seems to get him in the eye, brushes it away
and looks toward the ceiling.)
THAT LEAKS WHEN IT RAINS!
BERT AND ERNIE. *(Off.)*
NO BALUSTRADE BALLROOMS ...
MARY. *(Surprised.)* Bert and Ernie?

(GEORGE, who doesn't understand it either, shrugs,
nodding.)

BERT AND ERNIE. *(Off.)*
NO TOWERS OR THRONE.
GEORGE. *(Agrees.)* Not here! *(Sings.)*
NO BATHROOMS OR HALL ROOMS!
NO DOORKNOBS OR PHONE!

(GEORGE raises center shade to the top, revealing the
uniformed BERT and ERNIE, who stand shoulder to
shoulder, each holding his hat as in a formal
photograph. MARY can no longer resist laughing and
has to cover her mouth.)

THE THREE MEN. *(In all solemnity, as led by*
GEORGE.)*
THREE WALLS AND A CEILING!
MARY. *(Afraid she'll cry.)* I can't stand this!
GEORGE.
WE KNOW WE MUST FAIL!
THE THREE MEN.
THREE WALLS AND A CEILING!
GEORGE.
WE'RE SAFER IN JAIL!
BERT AND ERNIE. *(Hum.)*
AHHHH.
GEORGE.
THE PAINT IS ALL PEELING!

BERT AND ERNIE. (*Hum.*)
AHH-HAH! AHHHH.
GEORGE.
IT'S WARMER IN NOME!
But—
THE THREE MEN.
THREE WALLS AND A CEILING ...
IS HOME ... SWEET ... HOME!

(*MARY sits, a hand to her face as GEORGE nods his thanks to Bert and Ernie and pulls the shade down once again, the two disappearing behind it. HE goes to her.*)

MARY. (*Having enjoyed the whole thing but fearing he's displeased.*) ... How *could* you?
GEORGE. How could *you*? (*Makes a sweep of the place with his hand.*) Oh Mary!, it's wonderful—it really is. (*Then sits heavily, haunted by old ghosts.*) But—but I wanted so much more for you. I wanted the world!
MARY. (*Remembers.*) To see, to hear—

[Music #13: INTRO: ALL THE WORLD TO YOU]

MARY. —and to have it. (*Holds him tenderly against her breast.*) Oh, George, don't you know when I threw that rock—that was my wish *too*? (*Sings.*)

[Music #14: ALL THE WORLD TO YOU]

SO ...
SEE ME, HEAR ME,
AS YOU NESTLE NEAR ME.
DON'T TREAD LIGHTLY! KNOW ME
  THROUGH AND THROUGH!
TOUCH ME, TASTE ME,
WITH EVERY SENSE EMBRACE ME!

AND I PROMISE I'LL BE ALL THE WORLD TO
  YOU!

CHART MY OCEANS
RICH WITH DEEP EMOTIONS.
WHAT IF RAIN CLOUDS DRIVE AWAY THE
  BLUE?
MILD OR STORMY,
LOVINGLY EXPLORE ME!
AND I PROMISE I'LL BE ALL THE WORLD TO
  YOU!

THOSE MYSTERIOUS LANDS
THAT WOULD CALL US APART
ARE TONIGHT IN YOUR HANDS—
AS IS MY HEART.

SO ...
GENTLY, SWEETLY,
DEEPLY AND COMPLETELY,
LET IT TAKE A CENTURY OR TWO!
BODY, SOUL—
OH, BE MY MARCO POLO!
AND I PROMISE I'LL BE ALL THE WORLD—
YES, I WILL BE ALL THE WORLD—
(Extinguishes first candle.)
OH, MY DEAREST!, I'LL BE ALL THE WORLD
  TO YOU!

*(Extinguishes second candle and LIGHTS fall on the
  scene. At last, they rise on CLARENCE.)*

CLARENCE. *(Tugs at an ear, musing.)* I think ... that
girl really loves him.
JOSEPH. Well, she certainly had her chance to prove it.
In no time at all, it seemed ...

[Music #15: THE BAILEY WALK]

(MUSIC: Begin "The Bailey Walk," an instrumental, as LIGHTS drop on CLARENCE and rise on Main Street on a gorgeous spring day. BERT stands C., a whistle with a long, colorful lanyard in hand. HE directs unseen "traffic" as ERNIE lounges on a bench up right beside a sign that says, "Taxi Stand." GEORGE immediately enters L., wearing a suit and fedora, a pipe clenched in his teeth, looking proud as HE pushes a baby buggy—and VI simultaneously enters R., looking scrumptious, her clutch purse and hips swinging along.)

JOSEPH. There was one little Bailey ...

(BERT "stops traffic" to allow GEORGE and VI to pass him at C., GEORGE on the D.S. side, VI U.S., the TWO nodding to each other—and ERNIE happily observing. Once THEY're past him, BERT signals "traffic" to proceed.
First chorus ends as GEORGE and VI both exit—HE R. SHE L. Second chorus begins as GOWER enters R. and MARY enters left, also proud, pushing a much larger "double" buggy.)

JOSEPH. Two little Baileys ...

(The business is repeated at center, BERT stopping traffic to let MARY and GOWER cross, and then letting it proceed again as MARY exits R. and GOWER L.— simultaneous with end of second chorus.
Begin third chorus as UNCLE BILLY and MOTHER, walking together, enter L. and GEORGE and MARY enter R. brimming with good feelings—HE pushing the double buggy, SHE the smaller one.)

JOSEPH. Three little Baileys ...

(Again the business is repeated at C., UNCLE BILLY and MOTHER waving joyously to George and Mary as THEY cross. End third chorus as GEORGE and MARY exit L., UNCLE BILLY and MOTHER exit R.
Begin fourth chorus—but much slower in tempo as MARY and GEORGE, both looking bushed, enter L., SHE pushing the double buggy, HE the smaller one and carrying the actress who plays ZUZU—but who is dressed as a boy, wears a cap, and faces upstage.)

JOSEPH. Four little Baileys ...

(POTTER and P.M., who pushes him, enter R. GEORGE and MARY, seeing them, throw back their shoulders and—MUSIC resuming its original brisk tempo—the TWO, happy again, their energies renewed, strut proudly past Bert, Potter and P.M.
POTTER, having paused to look after them, reaches for Bert's whistle—which has yet to be blown—and blows it.)

POTTER. Stop!

(MUSIC, GEORGE, and MARY do exactly that, the two—who were just about to exit—turning to look back at Potter.)

POTTER. *(A general announcement.)* I *hate* the Bailey name!

(MUSIC completes last phrase, GEORGE and MARY strutting off as the CHILD that GEORGE carries sticks out her tongue and wiggles her fingers at the departing POTTER. BLACKOUT. LIGHTS rise on CLARENCE.)

CLARENCE. *(Musing over this last, pleased by it.)* Another true Bailey, I see.

JOSEPH. Clarence?

CLARENCE. I mean—You saw how—(*Is putting his thumbs in his ears to demonstrate—but as quickly stops, lest Joseph misunderstand.*) You know what I mean! (*Quickly, to change the subject.*) That—Potter. Was it really the Baileys he hated so much? Or was it the Savings and Loan?

JOSEPH. To Potter they were one and the same. You see, the Savings and Loan prospered during this time. George had convinced Sam Wainwright—

CLARENCE. (*Would display his knowledge.*) Old Hee Haw.

JOSEPH. Old Hee Haw—to install his new plastics factory in Bedford Falls, which made Sam wealthy.

CLARENCE. And George?

JOSEPH. George built and built—

CLARENCE. (*Delighted.*) Just as he said he would!

JOSEPH. But was barely getting by.

CLARENCE. (*Disappointed.*) Oh?

JOSEPH. Potter was really putting the pressure on, and what George built ... were good, solid, affordable homes—for people like Bert and Ernie—

CLARENCE. (*Proud of his knowledge.*) The cop and the cab driver.

JOSEPH. Yes—in a new subdivision called Bailey Park, allowing them to flee, for the first time, the so aptly named—Potter's field.

CLARENCE. (*Has to laugh.*) Hee hee hee!

JOSEPH. (*Surprised, curious.*) Clarence?

CLARENCE. (*Would wave him away.*) Oh—oh, never mind. I—I'm just—*imagining* how old man Potter ... (*Corrects himself.*) Mr. Potter, I *guess* I should say ... felt about that. (*Raises a hand.*) Don't! Don't do a thing, Joseph! (*Head lowered, eyes covered.*) I think—I can see and hear it—all by myself.

(*CLARENCE retreats into his imagination as LIGHTS fall on him and rise in Potter's office, a dark, disturbing room of lights and shadows, set to the L. of C. POTTER is behind a huge, high desk, poring over ledgers and receipts, the ever-present P.M. lurking behind him. Before the desk is a straight-backed wooden chair with a couple of inches sawed off its legs. All but in the shadows sits a lonely piano bench.)*

POTTER. (*Examining various receipts.*) Empty! ... Empty! ... (*Finds yet another one.*) ... Empty! (*Impales or "skews" the receipts on a paper skew, complains.*) How can I rent? How can I sell? When all of my tenants and clientele are moving to Bailey Park??? (*Looks at P.M., who returns his look with concern.*) Fool! (*P.M. reacts, hurt.*) Yes, you! Not me! You're letting me get excited. (*Checks his watch.*) And today of all days! (*Considers.*) I need something soothing ... loving. (*Growls.*) Quickly! The harpsichord,† you! (*P.M. goes to piano bench, sits facing the shadows, and begins to "play" a sort of minuet. We hear the pit piano, of course—which has been temporarily fitted with strips of paper to suggest a harpsichord sound, POTTER feeling much better, nearly relaxed.*) There's nothing like a love song ... when you're in a hateful mood.

[Music #16: I HATE YOU, GEORGE]

POTTER (*Sings—as delicately and deliciously as possible.*)
I HATE YOU, GEORGE.
I HATE YOU, GEORGE.
SINCE THAT FIRST DAY WE MET,
I'VE PICTURED YOU BESIDE ME AT
    NIAGARA FALLS ...
WHERE I'D PUSH YOU DOWN ...

---

† Potter may instead ask for a piano—in which case the business remains the same—or even a lute, lyre, zither, guitar, etc. especially if P.M. is actually able to play one of these instruments.

AND WATCH YOU DROWN.

I HATE YOU, GEORGE.
I HATE YOU. GEORGE.
AND HOW I'D LOVE TO GET
THE TWO OF US ALONE SOME NIGHT,
I'D SQUEEZE YOU IN MY ARMS SO TIGHT
I'D ADD NINE INCHES TO YOUR HEIGHT.
I HATE YOU, GEORGE.

("Dances" by turning chair to one side, then the other.)

TRA-LA-LA!
  P.M. *(Surprisingly.)*
HA-HA-HA!
  POTTER.
TRA-LA-LA!
  P.M.
HA-HA-HA!
  POTTER.
TRA-LA-LA!
  P.M.
HA-HA-HA! HA!

(POTTER has joined him at bench where P.M. has been playing with raptured abandon and one lavish knicks after another—their heads almost touching.)

  TOGETHER.
TRA-LA-LA, TRA-LA-LA, TRA-LA-LA, LA ...

(P.M. rises, the MUSIC continuing without him, and dances along with POTTER, working Potter's chair with turns and tilts as THEY sing:)

  POTTER.
TRA-LA-LA!

P.M.
HA-HA-HA!
    POTTER.
TRA-LA-LA!
    P.M.
HA-HA-HA!
    POTTER.
TRA-LA-LA!
    P.M.
HA-HA-HA, HA!
    POTTER.
TRA-LA!
(MUSIC rapidly changing.)
I AM NOT A SAINT BUT—A SINNER, BABY!
    P.M. *(Jolson-esque.)*
SINNERS, IF YOU NOTICE, ALL GO SOUTH!
    POTTER.
HOW I'D LOVE TO HAVE YOU—FOR
    DINNER, BABY!
    P.M.
I'D HELP YOU PLANT THE APPLE IN HIS—
    SASSY MOUTH!
    TOGETHER. *(THEY "sell" it, P.M. behind Potter.)*
WE'D BLIND YOU—
(P.M. kicks his left leg.)
WITH BLINDNESS.
(P.M. kicks his right leg.)
WE'D KILL YOU—
(Left leg.)
WITH KINDNESS.
(Right leg.)
    P.M.
LOVE AND HATE ARE TWO HEADS OF A
    COIN, YOU SEE—
    POTTER.
AND WHO KNOWS MORE ABOUT TWO-
    HEADED COINS THAN ME?

TOGETHER.
WE HATE—
(Now BOTH kick left legs.)
YOU—
(BOTH kick right legs.)
GEORGE!...

(THEY kick left, right, left, right, left, and finally right.)

P.M. *(When they are finished, resumes his modest, mortician-like character.)* That was ... very good, sir.

POTTER. *(Snarls, also resuming his.)* When I want your opinion, I'll ask for it. *(KNOCKING.)* There he is! *(P.M. quickly returns Potter to behind his desk. Now fatherly, kindly:)* Yes, yes—come in, my boy! Come in, George!

(GEORGE, almost at the age at which we first met him, enters and stops, not at all sure what he's doing here, hat in hand, ill at ease but polite. As HE continues across to Potter, we notice HE walks a bit more slowly, more deliberately, and there is a touch of gray in his hair.)

GEORGE. Uh ... Mr. Potter, I—

POTTER. *(Might be his dearest friend.)* Sit down! Have a cigar! Have a box of them!!!

GEORGE. *(Uncomfortable, actually below Potter in the sawed-off chair, GEORGE ignores the proffered box of cigars as HE looks for a place to set his hat, trying the edge of the desk, and then his knee.)* Well, sir—

POTTER. Now, now. Plenty of time to thank me later. *(Leans forward, compelling GEORGE's attention.)* George ...

GEORGE. Mr. Potter?

POTTER. *(Darkly excited.)* I have a proposition for you. *(Beat.)* Work for me.

GEORGE. (*Thunderstruck, turns right ear to Potter.*) Did—did I hear you right? (*Indicates left ear.*) That's my bad ear, y'know—Did you say, work for you? (*The hat is still a problem. GEORGE looks for a place to put it while POTTER laughs as if sharing a private joke with the grim P.M.*)

POTTER. Nothing so unusual about *that*! Why, I have hundreds in my employ and interests all over the globe! (*Leans in to press his advantage.*) You, George, would oversee them—travel extensively—bring your pretty little wife if you like. Take in the architecture of Rome, Cairo, Athens ... Frozen music, I believe the experts call it. (*Laughs.*) Yessir, Mr. George Bailey ... you'd see and hear the world! (*Train WHISTLE, GEORGE reacts.*)

GEORGE. Why, uh—

POTTER. Here's your contract. Top dollar, George! Ten times what you're making now! Why, your children, those four delightful *little* Baileys—hmm!—will attend the finest schools, get the start that was denied *you*— eh?—and never have to go hat in hand to anybody.

GEORGE. (*Embarrassed, and although POTTER doesn't seem to notice, puts his hat on the floor.*) Well, I don't—What about the Savings and Loan? What happens to *it*?

POTTER. (*Angry.*) Confound the Savings and Loan—! (*Catches himself.*) George, you've always been the best of the bunch! The smartest of the lot! (*Shrewd.*) And you've *known* it, too. (*GEORGE—who, heaven help him, has known it, reacts, and POTTER pretends a kind of grumbling warmth as he signals P.M. to the bench and pushes himself around the desk—to be closer to George.*) You've watched and even helped your classmates— people like Sam Wainwright without a fraction of your ability!—go on to rewarding careers—make a *fortune,* in Sam's case—while you've been stuck here nursemaiding (*Snarls.*) the "Savings and Loan"—an institution you hate almost as much as I do. (*GEORGE's head snaps up. Potter has his full attention.*) And now ... now ... you've

beaten me. There, I've said it! You've beaten old Henry Potter. After all these years of rapping each other, knocking each other, it's time—don't you think—we were just a little bit *kinder*? [Music #17: FATHERLY ADVICE] Me to you, George, you to me—and to your children, of course ... and Mary. (*Sings, P.M. "playing."*)
TAKE—WON'T YOU TAKE?
OH, TAKE—WON'T YOU TAKE
SOME FATHERLY ADVICE?
IT'S NICE TO BE GREAT,
SO NICE TO BE GREAT,
BUT GREATER TO BE NICE!

IT'S GOOD TO BE BEST—
BUT BEST TO BE GOOD.
    GEORGE. (*Speaks, still uncertain.*) You—wouldn' knock me?
    POTTER. Knock on wood!
(*WOODEN BLOCKS hit twice as he raps P.M.'s head.*)
MAKE NO MISTAKE.
FOR YOUR OWN SAKE, TAKE—
SOME—
    POTTER AND P.M. (*In harmony.*)
FATHERLY ADVICE...!
    GEORGE. Well, sir—(*GEORGE, starting to shake Potter's hand, feels a certain cold clamminess, and withdraws his own hand, looks at it and remembers who he is dealing with. To P.M.*) You, uh ... (*Nods for P.M. to play—and HE does, GEORGE singing.*)
GUESS I WILL TAKE,
AH, YES, I WILL TAKE
SOME FATHERLY ADVICE.
    POTTER. (*Thinks he's got him.*) Splendid!
    GEORGE.
WHEN AS A LAD
I WENT TO MY DAD,
HE SAID ... "A LOUSE BRINGS LICE."

POTTER. (*Unsure but alerted, P.M. all unawares, playing.*) He what?
GEORGE.
HE SAID TO BEWARE
THE PETTY AND SMALL.
POTTER. (*Speaks, to be certain.*) And—Henry Potter?
GEORGE.
MOST OF ALL!
SO YOU CAN SKEW—
(*Skews the contract on the skew; to P.M.*)
AND THAT GOES FOR YOU!—
YOUR—
GEORGE and P.M. (*P.M. remaining oblivious, harmonizes.*)
FATHERLY ADVICE!...

(*Putting on his hat, HE takes the cigar box and exits as*
   POTTER beats P.M. about the head and shoulders.
LIGHTS *down on office, up on CLARENCE.*)

CLARENCE. (*Still in his imagination, muses* a capella.)
TAKE, WON'T YOU TAKE?
OH, TAKE, WON'T YOU TAKE?
SOME FATHERLY AD—(*Warm, grins.*) Oh, I *like* that. (*Then, with concern.*) Did—did I do all right? Was that how it happened?
JOSEPH. (*A tad upset.*) No, Clarence, that was not at all the way it happened!
CLARENCE. (*Cowed.*) I—I've never exactly been known for my imagination, you see ...
JOSEPH. (*A grudging admission.*) Well—you got the gist of it. (*CLARENCE reacts, visibly relieved.*) George turned down an offer from Potter all right, and that Sunday, when he sat down to tell Mary—
CLARENCE. (*Anticipating.*) She was happy, I'll bet. She was proud of him.

JOSEPH. Somehow—the subject never quite came up. You see, they'd just started dinner ... when they learned the country had been attacked.

CLARENCE. (*Shocked.*) Attacked???

JOSEPH. (*Sadly.*) Yes.

[Music #18: WAR TABLEAU]

(Begin DRUM ROLL, which provides both the beat and some added emphasis for the following.)

JOSEPH. Suddenly they were busy like they'd never been before. The women went to work ... and the men went to War. Ernie won the purple heart, Bert the silver star. Harry, a Navy pilot, topped them all—by far.

CLARENCE. By far???

JOSEPH. He shot down fifteen enemy planes, two in hellbent dives toward an army transport ship. Saved a thousand lives.

CLARENCE. My gosh! (*DRUM ROLL buttons.*) And George? Did he fight too? (*Staunch, brave.*) Did he ... brave the cannon balls?

JOSEPH. (*Sighing.*) George fought—4 F because of his ear—the battle of Bedford Falls.

(SPOT hits GEORGE at C. apron, CLARENCE's LIGHT remaining up. GEORGE, carrying a flashlight and wearing a hard hat and an Air Raid Warden's arm band, turns immediately to face the spot.)

GEORGE. (*Hollers up.*) *Will you put that light out???* (*Semi-proud of himself, "spits" over his shoulder, reacts and mumbles, brushing imaginary saliva away as LIGHT drops.*) Doggone it ... (*CLARENCE, having observed this, turns again to Joseph.*)

JOSEPH. (*Continues, sadly.*) But if Bedford Falls was his battle ... Potter was his war.

CLARENCE. He must have really hated that.

JOSEPH. There was one ... who hated it more.

(LIGHTS out on CLARENCE, up in Potter's office, where POTTER sits grousing behind his desk.)

POTTER. (*As before.*) Empty! ... Empty! (*P.M. enters from left and waits to be recognized. Dully.*) What.

P.M. Mr. Bailey to see you, sir.

POTTER. (*Growls.*) *Which* Mr. Bailey? Slacker George?

P.M. The one everyone seems to call ... "Uncle Billy."

POTTER. (*Insult upon injury.*) That crazy old coot? Doesn't he know the war is over? If he comes in here one more time to brag about his nephew Harry—!

UNCLE BILLY. (*Off.*) They can't keep me out! (*Enters, wearing a hat and overcoat, carrying a newspaper.*) No sir, they can't keep me out! Well, Potter, old buddy, old bum! What do you have to say about *this*? (*Slaps newspaper down on the desk before Potter.*) The President! Yes, the President himself will, this morning, decorate Harry Bailey with—the Congressional Medal of Honor!

POTTER. (*Growls, sarcastic.*) Harry, ha? Not 4-F George?

UNCLE BILLY. (*Refuses to let Potter dampen his spirits.*) Only brought one paper, didn't I? Now if George had gone, he'd've won *two* medals! I'd've brought *two* papers! (*Giggles, pleased with himself.*)

POTTER. (*Pushes paper aside.*) Agghhh ...

UNCLE BILLY. Just can't keep those Baileys down, can you? No sir, you just can't keep those Baileys down! (*Exits, giggling, slapping his side.*)

POTTER. ... Burn this. (*Would hand P.M. the paper— but as HE extends it, a thick, business-size envelope drops out.*) Wait. (*Opens the envelope and stares, as does P.M. With the dark foreboding of new opportunity, POTTER looks up to meet P.M.'s eyes. THEY freeze.*)

(LIGHT rises on CLARENCE as HE regards the frozen tableau.)

CLARENCE. What is it? *(Turns to Joseph.)* What was in the envelope? *(LIGHTS fall on office scene. With all the foreboding derived from POTTER's gaze:)* Didn't that newspaper say—December twenty-fourth? *Today?* George's crucial day?! Tell me, Joseph—what did Uncle Billy leave behind?

JOSEPH. ... An entire week's receipts from the Savings and Loan. Several thousand dollars.

CLARENCE. *(Aghast.)* Oh no!

JOSEPH. Which, the government examiner being in town, Uncle Billy meant to deposit at the bank and forgetfully—

CLARENCE. *(Near anger as HE feels the impact of Billy's action.)* Foolishly!

JOSEPH. *(Sighs, would prefer a more charitable description.)* Perhaps. *(Then:)*—deposited with Potter instead.

(CLARENCE's LIGHT falls, LIGHTS rising D.S. only—with Potter's Office remaining set at L. and Zuzu's bedroom now preset at right. GEORGE, who wears no hat or overcoat, but has a long, dark scarf about his neck, prowls the area in anger, nearly distraught as HE attempts to retrace the steps of—and with—UNCLE BILLY who, still wearing his hat and overcoat, seems frantic and lost.)

[Music #19: WHAT A BREAK!]

OFF-STAGE CHORUS. *(Sing.)*
WHAT A BREAK! WHAT A BREAK!
WHAT A BREAK, GEORGE! WHAT A BREAK!
TO HAVE LOST—AND THOUGHT YOU HAD
WON!

WHAT A BREAK! WHAT A BREAK!
WHAT A MIS'RABLE MISTAKE!
AND THE COST—HAS NOT YET BEGUN!

GO TO JAIL! GO TO JAIL!
IT'S A SCANDAL! GO TO JAIL!
YOU'VE DISGRACED YOUR WHOLE
    FAMILY!...
GEORGE. (*Speaks, practically screaming at Uncle Billy.*) You stupid old failure! If there's to be jail, you're going—damn it!—not me!.... (*UNCLE BILLY retreats into the darkness.*)

[Music # 20: ONE LITTLE WORD]

GEORGE. (*Hurting more than he's ever hurt before in his life, turns D.S. and softly sings:*)
ONE LITTLE WORD ...
THREE LITTLE LETTERS ...
"WHY?"
(*Speaks.*)
Oh why?
(*Sings.*)
ONE LITTLE WORD
TWO LITTLE LETTERS ...
"ME?"
(*Speaks.*)
Oh my!
(*Looks up as to God, sings out, tortured.*)
YOU MUST HAVE HEARD
THOSE FIVE LITTLE LETTERS
AND FORGOT!
(*Then more quietly, in sorrow.*)
OR YOU REPLIED
WITH SIX LITTLE LETTERS ...
(*Speaks with irony.*)
 ... "Why not?" (*His head drops, his LIGHT falling as CLARENCE's rises.*)

CLARENCE. (*Not sure.*) A ... prayer?

JOSEPH. Of sorts. He couldn't let his uncle go to jail, and both men knew it. When George got home that evening, he screamed at his children, frightened his wife, and, if he'd had a dog, would have kicked it. He had endured one disappointment in life too many ... and felt very near the end of his rope.

CLARENCE. (*Hurting for George.*) Mary—couldn't help?

JOSEPH. He couldn't bring himself to tell her. All she knew was that for the first time in their married lives he'd been a miserable father to his children. She packed three of them off to her mother's while he went upstairs to see Zuzu—the only one in the house he was at all decent to ... (*Begin Zuzu's MUSIC as LIGHTS start up both on GEORGE—who has remained in exactly the position and attitude we left him in at C.—and in Zuzu's bedroom, where ZUZU lies, almost sitting up, on a small bed with a pink blanket, admiring a long-stemmed rose.*) and who had become ill that day when she ran home from school with her coat unbuttoned ... so proud she was of the big red rose she'd won.

[Music #21: DADDY, WON'T YOU FIX
MY FLOWER? (ZUZU)]

(*LIGHTS fall on CLARENCE as ZUZU sings, her voice causing GEORGE to turn to her.*)

ZUZU.
DADDY? WON'T YOU FIX MY FLOWER?

GEORGE. Hello, Zuzu. (*Having turned to her, HE moves closer and becomes part of her scene.*)

ZUZU.
DADDY? WON'T YOU FIX MY FLOWER?

GEORGE. ... I'll try. (*Sits on bed, takes it from her, unsure what to do.*)

ZUZU.
I KNOW THAT YOU GOT THE STRENGTH
   AND POWER ...
(SHE gives him several loose petals.)
DADDY? WON'T YOU FIX MY FLOWER?
*(Still unsure, HE pretends to try to affix the loose petals
   to the flower.)*
WON IT 'CAUSE I SANG A SONG!
(Rising, HE keeps his back to her as...)
SINCE THEN EVERYTHING'S GONE
   WRONG!
CAUGHT A LITTLE—
(SHE coughs daintily on beat...)
AND LOST SOME PETALS.
*(... and HE carefully inserts the loose petals into his
   watch pocket.)*
HOW COME THINGS CAN GO SO WRONG?
   GEORGE. *(Tortured.)* I don't know, honey—!
*(Knowing HE cannot unburden himself to her, HE
simply sits back down on the bed and hands her the
flower wordlessly.)*
   ZUZU. *(So pleased!, taking it.)*
DADDY? DID YOU FIX MY FLOWER?
   GEORGE. I—I think ...
   ZUZU.
DADDY? DID YOU FIX MY FLOWER?
   GEORGE. I tried.
   ZUZU.
I KNEW THAT YOU HAD THE STRENGTH
   AND POWER...
DADDY, OH YOU FIXED MY FLOWER!

*(HE embraces her, emotionally spent and ready to cry.
   SHE first gives him a warning...)*

   ZUZU. Daddy? *(Then, a scream.)* Daddy! *(HE leaps to
his feet and steps back as SHE shows him that his
embrace—which encompassed the flower—has caused*

her to detach a good part of the stem. Crying now.) You broke it! *(MARY enters, alerted by Zuzu's scream. SHE wears a house dress and apron and has reached the age at which we first met her.)* Mommy! He broke my flower! *(MARY steps between George and Zuzu.)*

MARY. *(Hurt, angry, protective.)* Must you torture the children???... Why don't you—*(As SHE speaks, SHE starts to point off, ready to tell him to leave, but snatches her hand back, frightened at the finality of the gesture.)*

GEORGE. *(Shocked, hurting more than his wife or daughter.)* ... Mary?... *(Can say no more, so apparent is the pain, anger, and fear in her eyes. HE takes another step back and turns away, closing his lapels against the cold, LIGHTS remaining up on him at D.S.C. as they fall on bedroom and rise on CLARENCE.)*

JOSEPH. With even Mary seeming to turn against him—

CLARENCE. *(Protests.)* Well, she did!

JOSEPH. So briefly, but ... *(In all honesty.)* Yes, perhaps she did. George felt he had but one chance to put things back together. *(LIGHTS rise partway in Potter's office. POTTER sits alone behind his desk, eyes on George's back, triumphant.)*

CLARENCE. *(Seeing POTTER, alarmed.)* Not—Potter!

JOSEPH. George had tried to call his one wealthy friend—Sam Wainwright—but he was in Europe and couldn't be reached ... So George told Potter he had lost the money but was ready to make it up—if Potter would only grant him a short-term loan. *(LIGHTS up full in Potter's office as CLARENCE turns to look, the LIGHT dropping on him.)*

POTTER. *(Feels better and better.)* *You* lost it, eh, George? *(GEORGE, on hearing Potter, turns to face him.)* Or ... did you *steal* it? It's all over town, you know, that you've been giving money to Violet Bick.

GEORGE. *(Protests.)* Mr. Potter—!

POTTER. *(Almost sweetly, HE is enjoying this so much.)* Oh, I know, I know. You "lent" her some—so she could leave town. (*Disgusted with him.*) Too bad, eh?, you didn't go with her.

GEORGE. If you'd just—! (*Produces an insurance policy.*) The—the one thing I have for collateral—

POTTER. (*Takes it.*) A *life* insurance policy? (*Examines it.*) Enough, I see, to cover the loss.

GEORGE. (*Uncomfortable.*) Well ...

POTTER. (*Shrewd.*) But what's the equity? What would you get if you cashed it in *now*?

GEORGE. Only a fraction of that, but—

POTTER. A *fraction*? And you'd use it as *collateral*?? For a loan from *me*??? (*A pause as HE realizes HE at last has won.*) Ha!!! (*P.M. enters from L. on hearing his master's voice.*) George, you once said I was frustrated ... Have you looked in the mirror lately...?

(*With a nod from POTTER, P.M. sits at bench and begins to "play" as POTTER speaks more than sings—in not nearly the brisk, joyous tempo of Uncle Billy's rendition, but taking the time to relish and twist each word.*)

[Music #22: ANOTHER FRUSTRATED MAN]

POTTER.
YOU'RE A FRUSTRATED MAN, MR BAILEY.
(*As GEORGE reacts.*)
Oh, you are.
YOU'RE A FRUSTRATED, ILL-TEMPERED
   BRAT.

NOW YOU'RE GOING TO JAIL—
AND YOU'LL NEVER MAKE BAIL.
BELIEVE ME!
OLD HENRY'LL SEE
TO THAT.
   P.M. (*Chuckles.*) He will!

POTTER.
YOU'RE A FRUSTRATED MAN, MR. BAILEY.
(As GEORGE turns.)
Don't look away!
(GEORGE, steeling himself, returns his gaze.)
ALL YOUR BRAINS, AND AMBITION, AND
   DRIVE—!

THOUGHT YOU'D BEAT ME AND THRIVE!
YOU WON'T EVEN SURVIVE!—

*(Pauses, all at once aware of the shattering significance of
what he is about to say. Even P.M. reacts with concern
as POTTER, singing the next lines with obvious
pleasure, pushes the insurance policy across to
George.)*

FOR YOU'RE WORTH
FAR MORE DEAD
THAN ALIVE!!!

[Music # 23: TIME TO SAY GOODBYE]

*(The significance is not lost on GEORGE either. HE
takes the policy, clutches it to his breast, and moves
down to center spot, LIGHTS dropping in Potter's
office.)*

GEORGE. *(Considers the words, frightened.)* Than ...
alive? *(TRAIN WHISTLE. HE reacts and then sings, the
words coming slowly, with none of the youthful abandon
he expressed earlier.)*
WHEN—I HEAR THE—WHISTLE OF A—
   TRAIN, MARY!
   MARY. *(Off.)*
SAVE HIM!

GEORGE. (*His reaction indicates he may—just may— have somehow heard the disembodied voice, his thoughts expressed in the next line:*)
IT CAN MAKE ME ALMOST GO—INSANE—
MARY! ...
ENSEMBLE.(*Off, louder.*)
SAVE HIM!
GEORGE. (*A greater reaction. LIGHTS—and SHADOWS—come up on Clarence's platform where— Clarence having left it—a railing has risen that suggests the structure of a bridge. VOICE and MUSIC building.*)
GOTTA GET OUT ... GONNA!...
TIME TO SAY GOOD BYE!...
CLARENCE. (*Off, overlapping George's last note.*)
Now, Joseph?
JOSEPH. Not quite.
GEORGE. (*Having arrived on the bridge, more quietly.*)
ONE LITTLE WORD ...
THREE LITTLE LETTERS ...
DIE.
ENSEMBLE.(*Off, simultaneous.*)
SAVE HIM!
GEORGE.
YES—
ENSEMBLE.(*Off, simultaneous.*)
SAVE HIM!
JOSEPH. (*Before GEORGE can sing his final "Die."*) Now, Clarence. (*GLISSANDO of a falling body, over which JOSEPH continues as GEORGE apparently "sees" the body fall.*) And good luck! (*SPLASH! GEORGE stares down into the water as:*)
CLARENCE. (*Off, screams.*) Help! I can't swim! Save me, George!

GEORGE. (*Immediately, both in shock and unsure he's heard right.*) What?
ENSEMBLE.(*Off.*)
SAVE HIM!!!

(So advised, GEORGE begins to tear off his jacket in an effort to save Clarence even as ENSEMBLE finish their last note. His action cues both a BLACKOUT and CODA.)

[Music #24: ACT I CURTAIN]

End of ACT I

ACT II

[Music #25: ENTR'ACTE]

Entr'Acte ends with all LIGHTS down. CURTAIN starts up on a dark stage and we hear:

[Music #26: WHAT A BREAK! #2]

OFF-STAGE CHORUS. (*Slower than the earlier brisk tempo, minor harmonics stressed.*)
WHAT A BREAK!... WHAT A BREAK!...

(LIGHTS rise at left in bridgetender's house. Towels, Clarence's clothes, and duplicates of George's hang on a line. GEORGE sits downstage in a blanket and a long underwear "dickey" which combine to conceal the suit and scarf HE actually wears beneath them. His hair is mussed, his head seems to ache, and HE holds a mug of coffee.)

OFF-STAGE CHORUS. (*Without pause.*)
WHAT A BREAK, GEORGE! WHAT A BREAK!
MUST YOU FAIL IN ALL THAT YOU DO?
GEORGE. (*Shifts uncomfortably, the song reflecting his thoughts.*) Oh boy.

(CLARENCE—heretofore hidden behind a pair of long towels, straightens to don an undershirt so ancient it seems more like a nightshirt, thereby catching GEORGE's—and our—attention.)

OFF-STAGE CHORUS.
HE'S A FAKE! HE'S A FLAKE!
THOUGH YOU SAVED HIM, NO MISTAKE,

HE INSISTS THAT HE HAS SAVED YOU!

CLARENCE. (*Sees GEORGE looking at him.*) George ... (*But GEORGE, not feeling at all communicative, waves Clarence off and looks away.*)

OFF-STAGE CHORUS.
KNOWS YOUR NAME, KNOWS YOUR GAME,
HE'S AN ODDBALL, ALL THE SAME,
A NUT THAT DROPPED FROM A TREE!...

(*CLARENCE tucks his shirt into his trousers—which are somewhat more modern than those we saw him in earlier—and approaches George.*)

CLARENCE. (*Speaks, diffident.*) Excuse—(*Coughs politely to get George's attention.*) my appearance. My name is Clarence Oddbody. (*Extends his hand for George to shake it.*) A.S.C. (*GEORGE, in a grim, self-hating mood, looks from the hand to Clarence and away.*)

GEORGE. (*Darkly.*) Oddbody. (*Then to Clarence, raising his voice.*) What's the A.S.C.?

CLARENCE. (*With no hint of embarrassment.*) Angel. Second Class. (*Confides.*) I'm your guardian angel.

GEORGE. (*Studying Clarence.*) You *look* like the kind of angel I'd get. Where're your wings?

CLARENCE. (*Cheerful, continues dressing.*) Oh, I haven't earned them yet. That's why I'm only second class ...

GEORGE. (*Marvels at Clarence's logic.*) Huh.

CLARENCE. (*Shows George his gold pocket watch and chain, shakes it to be sure it's dry.*) ... and, I suppose, why my watch doesn't work.

GEORGE. (*Doubtful.*) Your watch?

CLARENCE. That's what I do, make clocks and watches. (*Correction.*) I *did.* (*Proudly.*) I was working on *this* one just before I passed away. More than— (*Thinks.*) two hundred years ago.

GEORGE. (*Convinced he's dealing with a nutcase.*) Two hundred years, you say.

CLARENCE. (*Continues blithely.*) It's supposed to ring at noon and midnight—(*Stares at it.*) But it doesn't. Never did ... When a bell rings, y'see—that's when an angel gets his wings ... (*Sighs, confused but thoughtful.*) I expect that has something to do with it.

GEORGE. (*Wide-eyed, an exaggerated shrug.*) Could be. (*Would turn away, but CLARENCE persists.*)

CLARENCE. George ... you'll help me to get my wings, won't you?

GEORGE. (*Humors him.*) Sure, sure ... (*Then.*) How?

CLARENCE. By letting *me* help *you.* (*Continues to dress.*) You see, I know everything about you. Your boyhood, your ambitions, Mary, the missing money—

GEORGE. (*Attention caught.*) Now how could you know a thing like that? What are you, a mind reader or something?

CLARENCE. I told you! I'm your guardian angel. (*Confides.*) I *also* know killing yourself is not the answer.

GEORGE. Hey, I was only *standing* on the bridge. *You're* the one who jumped in.

CLARENCE. Because I knew *you'd* jump in, to save me. That's how *I* saved *you.* (*With some disappointment.*) I thought I already explained that. (*Returns to his theme.*) You see, without you—

GEORGE. (*Bitter.*) Without *me* everybody'd be a lot better off—is that what you want me to say? My wife, my kids, my friends ...

CLARENCE. (*Fully dressed now, upset at the idea, joins George D.S.C.*) No, no, I *don't* want you to say it! If you only knew all the good you've done! The wonderful life you've—(*Breaks off, something stirring in his memory.*) Wait—How did my mother used to put it? (*Remembers.*) Oh yes.

[Music # 27: IT'S A WONDERFUL LIFE]

(Sings.)
SOME SAY LIFE'S A FIGHT ...
THAT'S BETTER NOT BEGUN,
BUT WHEN YOU CARE FOR OTHERS ...
IT'S A FIGHT ALREADY WON.

NOT ONLY IS IT WON—
(Raises a finger.)
BUT DEAR AS IT CAN BE ...
(On "dear" raises a second finger.)
AND SO FULL OF BLESSINGS—!
(On "full" raises a third.)
IF YOU'LL COUNT THEM, YOU WILL SEE ...
(Again using his fingers to count.)
YES, IT'S A ONE, WON, TWO, DEAR, THREE,
    FULL LIFE!
A ONE, WON, TWO, DEAR, THREE, FULL
    LIFE!
IF YOU DON'T HAVE A STEAK,
YOU DON'T NEED A KNIFE,
IT'S A ONE, WON, TWO, DEAR, THREE,
    FULL LIFE!

IT'S A WONDERFUL, WONDERFUL,
    WONDERFUL LIFE!
A WONDERFUL, WONDERFUL,
    WONDERFUL LIFE!
IF YOU DON'T HAVE A DIME,
YOU DON'T NEED A WIFE,
IT'S A ONE, TWO, THREE, WONDERFUL,
    WONDERFUL LIFE!

WHEN WICKETS GET STICKY AND GOINGS
    GET TOUGH
YOUR ILLS AND BILLS AMOUNT—
WITH NO ONE TO COUNT ON, IT'S MORE
    THAN ENOUGH
TO KNOW YOU STILL CAN COUNT.

GEORGE. (*Having watched and listened in gloom.*) ... I count?

CLARENCE. (*Urges him.*) Please! (*Sings, signaling with his fingers.*)
IT'S A—

GEORGE. One.

CLARENCE.
WON.

GEORGE. Two.

CLARENCE.
DEAR.

GEORGE. Three.

CLARENCE.
FULL LIFE.
A—

GEORGE. One.

CLARENCE.
WON.

GEORGE. Two.

CLARENCE.
DEAR.

GEORGE. Three.

CLARENCE.
FULL LIFE.
IN VIEW OF THE FACTS,
IN SPITE OF THE STRIFE,
IT'S A—

GEORGE. One.

CLARENCE. Wondrous.

GEORGE. Two.

CLARENCE. So dear.

GEORGE. Three.

CLARENCE. Fulfilling? Yes, George—
A WONDERFUL LIFE!

GEORGE. (*With CLARENCE finished, after a pause, as glum and sarcastic as ever.*) Your mother actually sold you on that stuff, huh?

CLARENCE. (*Takes George's measure; to himself.*) This isn't going to be so easy...! (*To George, searching for a new tack.*) So you really think killing yourself will make everyone feel happier?

GEORGE. (*Considers.*) Oh, I don't know. I guess you're right. I suppose it'd've been better if I'd never been born at all.

CLARENCE. (*Shocked.*) What did you say?

GEORGE. (*Angry.*) I said I wish I'd never been born!

CLARENCE. There you go again! You—(*But has a thought.*) Wait. Just a minute now. *There's* an idea. (*Looks to the sky.*) What do *you* think? (*Listens.*) Yeah ... that'll do it. (*Smiles, nods, faces George.*) All right, George, you've got your wish!

(*THUNDER. BLACKOUT. The THUNDER continuing, "lost souls" in place, there are FLASHES of LIGHT from behind the scrim, L., R. and then C., until— flashes resolving, LIGHTS are full up behind scrim, revealing entire CAST [except GEORGE and CLARENCE] as dark, largely unrecognizable shadows in silhouette, most standing, some sitting, facing in various directions, and frozen in postures of despair as if they indeed were so many lost souls.*
A SPOT simultaneously rises down C. where, with the bridgetender's house struck, GEORGE, who is now fully dressed, stands with a cool, calm CLARENCE.)

GEORGE. (*Looks about.*) What—what happened?

CLARENCE. (*Points out.*) You're all dressed, George. (*Pause.*) You've never been born.

[Music #29: YOU'VE NEVER BEEN BORN]

(*As GEORGE reacts—first to his clothing, and then to the fact that HE seems to be able to hear out of his left ear:*)

CLARENCE AND CHORUS.
NO MORE LAUGHTER, NO MORE TEARS.
NO MORE FANCIES, NO MORE FEARS.
(GEORGE experimentally covers right ear to make sure.)
YOU CAN HEAR IN BOTH YOUR EARS!
GEORGE—YOU'VE NEVER BEEN BORN!
      GEORGE. *(Mutters.)* That's the strangest—
      CLARENCE AND CHORUS. *(As GEORGE, sensing that something is missing, checks side and rear pants pockets...)*
NO 4-F CARD, NO ID.
(... and then inside his jacket...)
NO INSURANCE POLICY.
(... and then, scared, his watchpocket.)
ZUZU'S PETALS CANNOT BE!
GEORGE—YOU'VE NEVER BEEN BORN!
(HE looks with alarm at Clarence.)
      CHORUS.
YOU'RE SAFE!
      CLARENCE. No longer will you fail.
      CHORUS.
YOU'RE FREE—
      CLARENCE. Won't have to go to jail.
      CHORUS.
TO NOT—
      CLARENCE. No family to rue.
      CHORUS.
—TO BE!
      CLARENCE. No friends. Not even *you!*
      CHORUS.
NO BANK—
      CLARENCE. And sure no S&L.
      CHORUS.
—RUPTCY!
      CLARENCE. No heaven and no hell.
      CLARENCE AND CHORUS.
PRAISE THE LORD, NOW YOU WILL SEE

WITHOUT YOU WHAT THE WORLD WOULD
    BE!

*(As GEORGE, frightened, steps back from Clarence,
    CLARENCE pursuing.)*

NO MORE PART IN POTTER'S PLOT.
NO LAMENTING AT YOUR LOT.
WHAT YOU SOUGHT IS WHAT YOU GOT!
    CLARENCE.
GEORGE—YOU'VE NEVER BEEN BORN!

    GEORGE. *(When THEY are finished, shaken.)* You
know something, Gabriel?

    CLARENCE. *(Reminds him, complaining.)* Clarence!

    GEORGE. You—you're *crazy!* I'm going home! *(Exits
spotlight, R.)*

    CLARENCE. *(Grins, a look to the sky.)* How'm I
doing, Joseph? *(Having apparently heard an answer.)
Thought* so. *(Exits spotlight, L. BLACKOUT.)*

[Music #29: YOU'VE NEVER BEEN BORN
            (TRANSITION)]

(In the BLACKOUT we hear, chillingly:)

    HARRY.
NO MORE LAUGHTER. NO MORE TEARS ...
    VI.
NO MORE FANCIES. NO MORE FEARS ...
    ERNIE.
NO 4-F CARD, NO ID ...
    MARY.
ZUZU'S PETALS CANNOT BE ...

*(LIGHTS rise both on the "lost souls" and on George's
    dining room—which we recognize because of the
    peculiar configuration of the shallow bay window area.
    But crimson curtains hang where we last saw posters*

*and shades, and a small nightclub-like table is occupied
by CLARENCE, who wears an overcoat and hat, his
back to us. At R. is a small, unoccupied bar.)*

GEORGE. *(Off and entering, L.)* Mary? ... Janey? ...
Mike? ... *(Looks about, stunned.)* Huh? Where'd those
curtains come from? That bar...?
CLARENCE. *(Swings around to face George.)* From
Potter, George. You didn't think he'd let a nice big house
like this go to waste???
GEORGE. *(Confused.)* To waste???

[Music #30: DADDY, WON'T YOU FIX
MY FLOWER? (VIOLET)]

(GEORGE reacts as we hear MUSIC and:)
VI. *(Moving for the first time, sings—with an
interpretation far different from that of Zuzu's.)*
DADDY? WON'T YOU FIX MY FLOWER?
GEORGE. *(Protests.)* That's Zuzu's song!
CLARENCE. *(Delicately.)* Not now. *(VI continues
around scrim and enters in a gown as red as the curtains.
SHE seems a chanteuse of sorts, her face etched in
hardness.)*
VI. *(Sells it, simmering.)*
DADDY? WON'T YOU FIX MY FLOWER?
GEORGE. *(Incredulous, on seeing her.)* Violet?
VI. *(Moves toward him...)*
I KNOW THAT YOU GOT THE STRENGTH
AND POWER...
*(... causing him, as HE backs away, to sit beside
Clarence.)*
DADDY? WON'T YOU FIX MY FLOWER?
GEORGE. *(Hisses to Clarence, upset.)* What's going
on here?
VI. *(Touches the two men as SHE sings, perhaps
ruffling Clarence's hair.)*
GAMBLED IT FOR JUST A SONG!

SINCE THEN EVERYTHING'S GONE
    WRONG!
CAUGHT A LITTLE—
(Not so much a cough as a coy "Ahem!" to avoid the
    missing word.)
AND LOST SOME PETALS.
HOW COME THINGS CAN GO SO WRONG?
(GEORGE starts to rise, but:)
    CLARENCE. *(A hand on George's arm, cautioning*
him.) Sit down.
    VI.
DADDY? WON'T YOU FIX MY FLOWER?
DADDY? WON'T YOU FIX MY FLOWER?
I KNOW THAT YOU GOT THE STRENGTH
    AND POWER ...
(Leans in close to George, voice low.)
Second room, upstairs.
(Pulls back, sings.)
DADDY, COME UP AND FIX MY FLOWER!
(Holds her position until song is finished, then exits and
    returns to lost souls.)
    GEORGE. *(To Clarence, shaken.)* I—I never saw
Violet act like that before.
    CLARENCE. You'll see a lot of things you never saw
before.

(ERNIE, who began to move when Violet finished,
    enters behind the bar.)

    ERNIE. *(Breezily apologetic.)* Sorry to keep you,
gents. We don't get a lot of customers Christmas Eve.
    GEORGE. *(Goes to him.)* Ernie! What's going on here?
    ERNIE. *(Fixes him with a hard look.)* Do you know
me?
    GEORGE. Do I—?! Of course I know you! You're
Ernie Bishop. You drive a cab. You live with your wife
and daughter in Bailey Park.
    ERNIE. *(A nerve struck.)* You seen my wife?

GEORGE. Seen her!? I've been over to your house a hundred times.

ERNIE. Look, Bub—I live in a shack in Potter's Field. My wife ran off and took the kid, and I ain't been behind a wheel since they pulled my license for drunk driving. Now do you want a drink or don't you?

GEORGE. (*Sits at bar, more shaken.*) A—a double bourbon. (*CLARENCE, beside him, clears his throat.*) ... One for him too.

ERNIE. (*Mutters.*) That's more like it. (*Starts to fix drinks.*)

GEORGE. Ernie ... is—is this some kind of a dream? Where am I? Right now.

ERNIE. Pottersville. Where'd you think?

GEORGE. (*Confused.*) You mean Bedford Falls.

ERNIE. I mean Pottersville. I oughta know where I live!

(*GEORGE looks toward the scrim, startled, as—some of the LOST SOULS turning to face U.S.—their back light drops and LIGHTS come up on a new drop: Pottersville. It is a night scene, winter, very much resembling the Bedford Falls drop—but twisted, garish and lusty. Bars, dance halls and strip joints stand where other businesses once stood. The church is gone and, perhaps most telling of all, the water tower is marked: "Pottersville." GEORGE turns to Ernie as drop LIGHT falls, the lost souls back lit as before.*)

GEORGE. (*Demands.*) This address! What's the address of this ... house?

ERNIE. 320 Sycamore. (*GEORGE reacts.*) Got a problem with that?

GEORGE. (*Hurting, and so quiet ERNIE can scarcely hear him.*) I... I *live* here.

ERNIE. (*Serves the drinks but, put off by GEORGE's strange reactions:*) You got the dough to pay for this?

GEORGE. (*Automatically.*) Sure, sure. (*Wolfs his drink down.*)

CLARENCE. (*A gentle reminder.*) No you don't, George.

GEORGE. (*Realizes, touching his pocket.*) What? Oh ... (*Tries to explain to the hard-eyed ERNIE.*) I—well, I—I jumped in the river just now, and I guess I must've lost all of my— (*Gives up on this, looking desperately at Clarence.*)

CLARENCE. Don't look at *me*. I *never* carry money.

ERNIE. (*Has had it.*) That's it. (*Slaps a bartop BELL with the palm of his hand.*)

CLARENCE. (*As swift as a "gesundheit."*) Thank you.

ERNIE. (*Glowers.*) What?

CLARENCE. You rang a bell, an angel got his wings ... (*Content.*) One of my friends, I expect. (*ERNIE, concerned, hits BELL again.*) Thank you. (*And again.*) Thank you. (*And again.*) Thank you.

ERNIE. (*Mutters, looking about.*) Where's that part-time bouncer? (*BERT appears at L. in uniform.*)

BERT. You want me, Ernie?

ERNIE. (*Unable to find the proper words.*) These— these two—

GOWER. (*Off.*) M-merry Christmas! (*Enters R. almost unrecognizable. HE's unshaven, unshorn, messy, and probably smells. His mind all but gone, HE wears an idiot's grin as HE does his best to keep up appearances.*) Merry Christmas to you! I—I hoped, for the sake of the season—

GEORGE. (*Shocked.*) Mr. Gower!

BERT. (*Who is no less large and more than a touch harsher in this existence, starts for him.*) Rummy, didn't I tell you never to come panhandling here?

GEORGE. (*Gets there first.*) Wait, Bert. Mr.—Gower? It's me, George Bailey ... You know me, don't you?

GOWER. (*Progressively frightened, backing off.*) No!... No!... No!...

BERT. Out you go! (*Takes Gower by the collar and seat of the pants, gives him the bum's rush off.*)

GEORGE. (*Can't believe what HE's seen, turns to Ernie.*) Ernie! Wasn't that Mr. Gower? The druggist?

CLARENCE. It *was* Gower, George. After twenty years of prison.

GEORGE. Prison?

CLARENCE. (*Simply.*) He poisoned a child.

ERNIE. (*Remembers.*) Geez, I forgot about that.

GEORGE. (*Would protest.*) But—!

CLARENCE. (*Regards George sadly.*) Y'see, you weren't there to stop him.

GEORGE. (*Insists.*) But I did stop him! I remember distinctly!...

(*BERT returns, wiping his hands.*)

BERT. (*To Ernie, dour.*) Now what?

ERNIE. (*Points, still behind his bar.*) These two ... Just get rid of 'em.

BERT. OK ... (*Starts for GEORGE, who backs off.*)

GEORGE. Wait ... Wait, Bert ... You've gotta understand. This is my house! (*BERT reaches for him but GEORGE, backpedaling, CRASHES a chair between them.*)

BERT. OK, if you won't come quietly ... (*Takes out his blackjack.*) Ernie? (*ERNIE, braver with Bert in the picture, comes around the bar with a baseball bat.*)

ERNIE. (*Cautions George.*) Better do like he says.

GEORGE. (*Progressively cornered.*) Bert ... Ernie ... I beg of you. Don't—

BERT. (*Lifts his blackjack, ready to strike.*) Sorry, pal...

CLARENCE. (*Raises a hand.*) Freeze. (*A swift, tinkling, ascending GLISSANDO, the THREE FREEZING just as GEORGE is about to get swatted. CLARENCE, who is, after all, new at this, shakes his head in disappointment.*) ... Not *you*, George.

(*GEORGE comes to life, sees the TWO OTHERS are frozen.*)

GEORGE. Huh?

CLARENCE. Come on! Let's go. (*Takes George's sleeve, explaining.*) I'm not sure how long they stay that way.

(*HE and GEORGE exit L. As soon as they're gone, a descending GLISSANDO, BERT and ERNIE coming to life, BERT swinging his blackjack, its natural arc causing him to hit himself in the knee.*)

BERT. Ye-ouch! (*Looks all about.*) Where—where did they go?

ERNIE. (*Even more shaken than Bert.*) I think I need a—

BERT. So do I. (*Joins ERNIE at bar, inadvertently ringing BELL.*)

ERNIE. (*Jumps, nerves shot.*) Don't do that! (*As BERT stares at him, puzzled.*) You just gave some friend of theirs his—(*But realizes he's already said too much.*) I'll explain later. (*Wolfs down Clarence's untouched drink and pours another, a nonplused BERT staring and staring at him as the LIGHTS fall.*)

[Music #31: WHAT A BREAK! #3]

CHORUS. (*In the dark.*)
WHAT A BREAK! WHAT A BREAK!
WHAT A BREAK, GEORGE! WHAT A BREAK!
FOR IT SEEMS YOU DO NOT EXIST!

WHAT A BREAK! WHAT A BREAK!
WHAT A BREAK! GOODNESS SAKE!
SO NOW YOU'LL NEVER BE MISSED!

(LIGHTS up on lost souls and D.C. GEORGE, hands jammed in his pockets, braced against the cold, enters with CLARENCE.)

ALL AROUND YOU APPALLS.
WHERE IS OLD BEDFORD FALLS?
AND WHERE ARE THE FRIENDS YOU ONCE
    KNEW?...

CLARENCE. *(Speaks, explaining.)* Though you haven't failed ... still, Potter's prevailed. *(Sighs.)* I hope I've at last gotten through.
GEORGE. *(Turns on him.)* Cut it out, cut it out, will you? You—! What are you? Are you a hypnotist?
CLARENCE. *(Shakes his head, grinning.)* No.
GEORGE. You—you've got me seeing things here. *(Determined.)* I know *one* person who'll know me—and I know where to find her, too!
CLARENCE. *(Anticipated this.)* ... Your mother?
GEORGE. *(Screams, afraid he may be wrong.)* YES!
CLARENCE. *(Sighs.)* George, you don't have a—
GEORGE. *(Warns, ready to strike Clarence if he has to.)* Shut up! Stop it! Get out of here!

(CLARENCE gives it up for the moment and exits L. As GEORGE watches him out, a doorway—not a door, but a doorway with a sign saying "Ma Bailey's Boarding House"—swings out from R. GEORGE turns, goes to it, reads the sign, and, as HE hesitates to knock, MOTHER appears in doorway. Ill-treated by life, SHE seems a dried-up, unpleasant, even shrewish old woman, far from the loving, energetic soul we knew.)

MOTHER. *(Challenges, suspicious.)* What do *you* want?
GEORGE. *(A hard time believing it's she.)* Mother?

MOTHER. (*Twists the word, unaccustomed to it.*) *Mother!*?

GEORGE. Don't you know me? It's George!

MOTHER. (*Wants to be rid of him.*) George who? I never saw you before in my life. If you're looking for a room—

GEORGE. Something—something *terrible* has happened to me. If—if you'll just take me in till I can get over it ...

MOTHER. (*Blocks his passage, misunderstanding.*) I don't take in boarders unless they're recommended by people I know.

GEORGE. But—but I know *everyone* you know! (*Grasps at a straw.*) Your brother-in-law, Billy!

MOTHER. (*Surprised he should say this, but shrewd.*) Oh? When'd you see him last?

GEORGE. Just this morning. At work!

MOTHER. Liar! He had a stroke when he lost his business. He's buried in Potter's Field beside my husband. (*Pause.*) And my son! (*Exits, angry, lest she break down and cry—and thereby lose the terrible hardness that has become her protective shell.*)

GEORGE. (*Protests.*) Your *son*? But *I'm* your ...

(*SPOT rises on CLARENCE D.C. —where HE stands behind three small grave markers.*)

CLARENCE. She wasn't talking about *you*, George. She was talking about Harry. (*GEORGE goes to him, LIGHTS dropping on doorway.*) Don't you see? (*Indicates marker.*) Harry Bailey died when he fell through the ice at the age of nine.

GEORGE. (*Ignores the evidence in his outrage.*) That's a lie! Harry Bailey went to war! He won the Congressional Medal of Honor! He saved the life of every man on that transport!

CLARENCE. (*So sadly.*) Every man on that transport *died*. Harry wasn't there to save *them*—because *you* weren't there to save *Harry*. (*GEORGE falls on his knees before the marker, covers his face with hands.*)

[Music #32: INCIDENTAL: HARRY'S GRAVE]

CLARENCE. (*Continues gently.*) Isn't it strange!... Each life touches so many others. When there is just one missing ... it can leave an awful hole. (*Moves in closer, wants to touch George's shoulder, but restrains himself from doing so.*) Don't you see what a terrible thing it would be ... to throw yours away? (*MUSIC out as GEORGE slowly lowers his hands, at last accepting Clarence for who he is.*)

GEORGE. Clarence ... Where's Mary?

CLARENCE. (*Dissembles.*) Oh! Well, I—

GEORGE. (*On his feet, insists.*) Somehow you know these things! Tell me where she is.

CLARENCE. (*Protests.*) I'm not supposed to!

GEORGE. (*Takes him by the lapels, threatening.*) Tell me! I've got to see her!

CLARENCE. (*Would spare him.*) You—you won't like it, George. She never married. She's an old maid.

GEORGE. (*Forces CLARENCE to stand on his toes as he lifts him by his lapels, ready to commit violence.*) Tell me!!!

CLARENCE. (*At last.*) She's ... just closing the library. (*GEORGE releases CLARENCE, who falls to the floor, and rushes off R. CLARENCE rises, shaken but philosophical.*) I—I guess—if there were an easier way to earn wings—more folks would probably have 'em. (*Sighs, scratches his head, and replaces his hat. BLACKOUT.*)

[Music #33: WHAT A BREAK! #4]

CHORUS. (*In the dark.*)
WHAT A BREAK! WHAT A BREAK!
WHAT A BREAK! WHAT A BREAK!

WHAT A TOUGH PILL TO TAKE!...
WHAT A BREAK, GEORGE!...
(And, at last, ending.)
WHAT A BREAK!...

*(Lights up D.S., lost souls no longer in evidence, as
MARY enters from left. SHE seems older than ever,
and tight-lipped from days and nights of loneliness.
Her hair is combed back into a severe bun. SHE wears
glasses, a mannish hat, much too sensible shoes, and a
gray suit. GEORGE quickly enters from R.)*

GEORGE. *(Stops dead, seeing her.)* Mary! *(Startled,
not recognizing him, SHE tries to go around him. But HE
moves with her and takes her arms.)* Mary! I was sure
you'd know me.
MARY. *(A frightened but firm denial.)* ... No!
GEORGE. *(Her denial destroying his one last hope, HE
releases her, mumbling an apology.)* Forgive me ... I—I
guess I mistook you for someone else. *(Turns away in
despair.)*
MARY. *(However, does not move. HE seems so
pitiful and a puzzling question has occurred to her.)* And
her name was Mary ... *(Shocked to realize SHE's still
there, HE faces her and SHE adds—quite an admission.)*
too?
GEORGE. *(Moved by her kindness.)* If—if only you
could remember—!

[Music #34: ALL THE WORLD TO YOU (REPRISE)]

GEORGE. *(Sings.)*
HOW YOU WANTED ME TO
SEE YOU, HEAR YOU,
ALWAYS TO BE NEAR YOU!
*(SHE turns away, in her own way as desperate as HE is,
his every word troubling her as SHE tries to
understand the strange feelings they evoke.)*

I WAS YOUNG—AND YEARNING TO BE
   FREE!
(Approaches but does not touch her.)
THOUGH I KNEW THAT I WOULD
NEVER LEAVE YOU,
WHY DIDN'T I BELIEVE YOU ...
WHEN YOU PROMISED—YOU'D BE ALL THE
   WORLD TO ME?
   MARY. *(Terribly disturbed, **these** last words sounding
so familiar!, and feeling an affinity towards this man that
she has never felt towards another, SHE steps forward to
avoid meeting his eyes.)* But—but I ... *(Dares to sing, at
last turning to him.)*
ONLY REMEMBER THAT I
HOPED FOR—
   GEORGE. *(Encourages.)*
HOPED FOR?
   MARY.
PRAYED FOR—
   GEORGE.
PRAYED FOR?
   MARY.
THE ONE MAN I WAS MADE FOR!
(Bittersweet.)
ALL THOSE GREEN YEARS—MY, HOW FAST
   THEY FLEW!
AND OF COURSE THERE WERE SOME
PARTIES ...
   GEORGE.
PARTIES?
   MARY.
KISSING ...
   GEORGE. *(Very close to her.)*
KISSING?
   MARY.
BUT WITH THAT ONE MAN MISSING—
(Sad, almost accusing.)

HOW COULD I PROMISE—I'D BE ALL THE
    WORLD TO YOU?
    GEORGE.
IT TOOK SO LONG TO SEE!
I'VE BEEN SENSELESS AND NUMB!
ALL YOU PROMISED TO BE ...
YOU HAVE BECOME!
IF I'VE
NEVER ...
    MARY.
NEVER!
    GEORGE.
TOLD YOU ...
    MARY.
NEVER!
    GEORGE.
HOW I LOVE TO HOLD YOU!—
(HE moves toward her but SHE moves away.)
I DIDN'T KNOW WHAT LOSING YOU
    WOULD BE!
    MARY. *(Faces him to plead.)*
CAN'T YOU SEE I JUST REMIND YOU—
    GEORGE.
REMIND ME?
    MARY.
OF HER?
    GEORGE. *(Wondering if she may be right.)*
OF HER?
    MARY.
IF YOU REALLY LOVE HER—
    GEORGE. *(Speaks, quietly.)* Oh, I do.
    MARY.
WHY DIDN'T YOU TELL HER,
"YOU ARE ALL THE WORLD—"
    GEORGE.
I SHOULD HAVE TOLD YOU ...
YOU ARE ALL THE WORLD—!
(Speaks.)

Or is it too late to say ...

TOGETHER.
YOU ARE ALL THE WORLD TO ME!
(THEY hold—facing but not touching each other until:)

GEORGE. *(Takes her in his arms.)* Mary—it can't be too late!

MARY. *(Struggles—) No!... (—and pushes away, crying, nearly hysterical, whatever spell he held her in broken.)* I told you—I DON'T KNOW YOU! *(Rushes off, BERT entering.)*

BERT. It's OK, lady—I *do.*

GEORGE. *(As BERT reaches for him.)* Bert, I hate to do this—*(Slugs him and rushes off L.)*

BERT. *(Who has fallen to one knee, calls, homicidally angry.)* You're dead! You hear me? You're *dead! (Rises and starts after George. BLACKOUT. We hear the WIND and:)*

[Music #35: INCIDENTAL: BACK TO THE BRIDGE]

GEORGE. *(In the dark, calls.)* Clarence!... *(LIGHTS up on bridge scene as before, GEORGE not yet having entered lighted area. Off, closer.)* CLARENCE!... *(Arrives on bridge, looks about, more desperate than ever.)* Help me, Clarence! Get me back! Get me back to her! *(Police SIREN.)* Get me back to my wife and kids! They're all I care about! I don't care what happens to me! Get me back! I want to live! *(SIREN winds down. With realization.)* I want to live! *(A car door SLAMS.)* I want to live again! Help me! *(Drops his head onto his clenched fists, the most deeply felt prayer he's ever said.)* Dear God!... Let me live again. *(The WIND we heard ceases. BERT enters light frame.)*

BERT. There you are!

GEORGE. *(Turning, sees him, warns.)* Stay away from me, Bert! I'll hit you again!

BERT. (*Confused.*) What the Sam Hill are you talking about? Mary's had me looking all over town for you, George!

GEORGE. (*As HE gets it.*) Mary??? George??? (*Touches him to be sure he's real.*) Do you know me, Bert? Did you call me George?

BERT. (*Uneasy at the touching and GEORGE's extreme happiness at seeing him.*) Sure I did. What are you, deaf?

GEORGE. (*Realizes, excited.*) Bert! I *am* deaf! (*Indicates left ear.*) *I can't hear a thing out of this ear!!!* (*As BERT stares, GEORGE checks watchpocket and takes petals out.*) Zuzu's petals! Hot dog!

BERT. (*Not at all sure what's going on, would explain his mission.*) I had to come get you on account—

GEORGE. (*Too happy for such staid things as explanations, interrupts him.*) That's it! Count!

BERT. (*Confused.*) Count?

GEORGE. (*More sober, persuasive.*) Please.

[Music #36: FINALE]

(*Sings.*)
IT'S A—
(*Holding up fingers as CLARENCE did for him:*)
　　BERT. (*Lost but game.*) One.
　　GEORGE.
WON.
　　BERT. Two.
　　GEORGE.
DEAR.
　　BERT. Three.
　　GEORGE.
FULL LIFE.
(*Getting more excited, tempo increasing, as BERT gets the hang of it.*)
A—
　　BERT. One.

GEORGE.
WON.
   BERT. Two.
   GEORGE.
DEAR.
   BERT. Three.
   GEORGE.
FULL LIFE.
(Shows a dime from his pocket.)
I'VE GOT A DIME!
(ANOTHER REALIZATION, EXCITED.)
AND I'VE GOT A WIFE!
IT'S A WONDERFUL—
(BERT joining in.)
WONDERFUL, WONDERFUL LIFE!

(GEORGE turns away from BERT as LIGHTS rise in his living room—that is, full stage including night winter scene of the restored Bedford Falls. Sheer white curtains hang in the window area where MARY stands with ZUZU in her arms before the dining room table— which holds several small glasses. The TWO sing directly to GEORGE, who goes to them, the LIGHT dropping on BERT.)

   MARY.
IT'S A BEAUTIFUL—
   ZUZU.
BEAUTIFUL—
   MARY AND ZUZU.
BOUNTIFUL BALL!... *(Hold MUSIC as GEORGE embraces and kisses them.)*
   GEORGE. Mary! Mary! Zuzu!
   ZUZU. I'm much better, Daddy!

(MOTHER enters R. excited, producing a wad of cash from her open purse to show to George.)

MOTHER.
SO MANY ANSWERED MARY'S CALL!...
GEORGE. (*Delighted to see her.*) Mother!

(*UNCLE BILLY enters behind her with a laundry basket
that's full to overflowing with paper money.*)

UNCLE BILLY.
SHE SAID, "GEORGE NEEDS HELP!"
AND THAT SAID IT ALL! (*Deposits basket on
table as:*)
GEORGE. (*Reacts.*) Uncle Billy!
MARY, ZUZU, MOTHER AND UNCLE BILLY.
IT'S BEAUT OF A BEAUTIFUL, BOUNTIFUL
BALL!

(*GOWER enters. Like the others, HE has again become
the person we knew.*
*Note that during the following, UNCLE BILLY will take
a wine bottle from the basket, open it, mime filling the
glasses and, with the help of the others, make sure that
everyone but ZUZU gets one.*)

GOWER. (*MUSIC continuing without pause.*)
I CABLED SAM WAINWRIGHT AND ASKED
   HIM TO DRAW
SOME CASH FROM HIS ACCOUNT.
GEORGE. (*So happy to see him.*) Mr. Gower!
GOWER.
HE CABLED RIGHT BACK:
(*Reads from the cablegram in his hand.*)
"IF GEORGE NEEDS IT—HEE HAW!—
I'LL PLEDGE THE FULL AMOUNT!"

(*VI, who has just entered, drops a few dollars into the
basket.*)

VI. (*Quietly, to George.*) Good old Sam!

GEORGE. (*Reacts, happy.*) Vi!
ALL. (*Sing in various parts.*)
IT'S A WONDERFUL LIFE!
A WONDERFUL LIFE!
IN VIEW OF THE FACTS,
IN SPITE OF THE STRIFE,
IT'S A—
(*But ERNIE enters with an announcement.*)
ERNIE. Harry Bailey!!! (*MUSIC OUT as there are "Ohhh's" and a smattering of APPLAUSE—actually, hands clasped together in joy—as HARRY, handsome as ever in his Navy pilot's uniform, enters behind ERNIE, who explains, sotto voce, to Gower.*) Darn fool flew all the way up from Washington in a blizzard. I got him here as quick as I could.
GEORGE. (*Staring, his cup running over, ready to cry, and so quietly we may have difficulty hearing him.*) Harry!... Harry!...
HARRY. (*Takes a glass from Uncle Billy.*) Good idea, Uncle Billy. (*Holds the glass high, grins.*) To my big brother George ... the richest man in town.

(*Various ad libs of "To George!," "Hear, hear!," etc., as THEY raise their glasses high. ZUZU, who has no glass and has been looking into the basket, lifts her hand as the others do—in a "toast"—and out comes Clarence's gold watch and chain.*
MUSIC, the others clinking their glasses, ZUZU studying the watch, and then showing it to her mother—as BERT and POTTER'S MAN enter with an enormous, already decorated Christmas tree which THEY carry to L. As BERT plugs it in, POTTER'S MAN diffidently approaches George, peels a dollar off a small roll of bills, hands it to him, and then, figuring what the heck, gives him the whole roll.
Following HUZZAHS and APPLAUSE as THEY react to the lighted tree:)

UNCLE BILLY. (*Sings.*)
WHO SAVED THE BAILEY SAVINGS AND
LOAN?
THE OTHERS.
SAVE GEORGE! SAVE GEORGE!
ERNIE.
WHO BRAVED AN ANGRY MOB ON HIS
OWN?
THE OTHERS.
BUT GEORGE! OUR GEORGE!
MARY. (*Who has accepted the watch from Zuzu,
curious about its inscription.*)
WHO HAS AN INSCRIPTED WATCH, OF ALL
THINGS?
(*Holds it close to read.*)
"WAIT TILL CHRISTMAS."
GEORGE. (*Starts to understand.*) Hey!
MARY. (*Continuing.*)
"THAT'S WHEN IT RINGS."
UNCLE BILLY. (*Checks his own watch.*) It's
Christmas.

(*George's watch RINGS so loudly it startles everybody.
Led by UNCLE BILLY, there are various ad libs of
"Merry Christmas!"*)

GEORGE. (*Now fully understanding, comes forward.*)
WHOSE GUARDIAN ANGEL ... JUST GOT
HIS WINGS?...
(*Raises his glass to heaven.*) Attaboy, Clarence.
MARY. (*Ready to believe anything her man says.*) If
you say so. (*Raises her own glass.*) Attaboy. (*Exchanges
looks and grins with GEORGE as:*)
ALL. (*Save GEORGE, who's much too busy
grinning—those with glasses holding them high.*)
SAVE ... SAVE GEORGE!...

ALL. (*Including GEORGE, dance and sing in various parts.*)
IT'S A WONDERFUL LIFE!
IT'S A WONDERFUL LIFE!
IF YOU DON'T HAVE A STEAK
YOU DON'T NEED A KNIFE!
IT'S A ONE, TWO, THREE, WONDERFUL
   LIFE!

(*As THEY begin SECOND CHORUS, CLARENCE enters, dressed in a spotless white gown and the biggest, most graceful, most beautiful pair of wings you've ever seen. The OTHERS are oblivious to him, of course, as HE proudly crosses the stage and mounts his platform.*)

ALL. (*But CLARENCE, sing in various parts.*)
IT'S A WONDERFUL LIFE!
IT'S A WONDERFUL LIFE!
IF YOU DON'T HAVE A DIME,
YOU DON'T NEED A WIFE!
IT'S A ONE, TWO, THREE, WONDERFUL,
   WONDERFUL, WONDERFUL LIFE!

(*GEORGE and MARY dance, watched by the OTHERS as:*)

CLARENCE. (*Who has mounted his platform and stands beside the tree, sings:*)
NO MATTER HOW OFTEN, NO MATTER HOW
   FAR,
TO FALL IS NOT TO FAIL.
NO MATTER HOW FRAIL AND FRIGHTENED
   YOU ARE,
TO LOVE IS TO PREVAIL!
   THE OTHERS.
WONDERFUL WONDERFUL WONDERFUL
   WONDERFUL LIFE!

ABOUT HALF THE CAST.
IT'S A WONDERFUL, WONDERFUL,
   WONDERFUL LIFE!
A WONDERFUL, WONDERFUL,
   WONDERFUL LIFE!
THE OTHER HALF. (*Simultaneous.*)
SHOULD AULD ACQUAINTANCE
BE FORGOT!
   MARY AND GEORGE. (*Surrounded by their loved
ones, raise their glasses to each other.*)
AND I PROMISE I'LL BE ALL THE WORLD TO
   YOU!
(*THEY link their arms as if prepared to drink, but kiss
   as:*)
The Others. (*Including CLARENCE.*)
A WONDERFUL LIFE!!!

(*As THEY hold the final note, CLARENCE places a
   winged angel atop the Christmas tree.*)

CURTAIN

[Music #37: BOWS]

PROPERTY PLOT and SOUND EFFECTS

ACT I

Opening
Pocket watch (Clarence)
After the Prom
Preset—
Cardboard cutout bush (and Violet!)
One "sopping" bundle each (George and Mary)
First S&L Scene
Preset—
Uncle Billy's desk and chair
Potter's wheel chair (mentioned only here; Potter—as Potter—always has wheel chair)
"Tuition" envelope (George, second entrance)
Wedding Reception
Preset—
Bench, two chairs, white picket fence, table with a whiskey bottle and several "pitched" glasses
Pocket bottle (Uncle Billy)
Travel folders (George)
Money Scene
Preset—
Uncle Billy's desk and chair
One large black umbrella each (Dancers)
Sheaf of banknotes (Mary)
Honeymoon
Preset—
Wagon with three-part window frame hung with shades decorated with travel posters, the center shade "working" (able to roll up and down); the wagon also holds two chairs and a dining room table with linen cloth, china, covered entreé, two unlit candles, matches, and a candle-snuffer
Bailey Walk
Preset—
"Taxi Stand" sign and bench
Whistle with a long, colorful lanyard (Bert)
Pipe, small buggy (George)
Double buggy (Mary)
First Potter's Office Scene
Preset—

Large desk with ledgers, receipts, paper skew, contract and cigar box
Sawed-off chair
Piano bench
(Optional: harpsichord "shell")
War Tableau
Flashlight, hard hat, Air Raid Warden arm band (George)
Second Potter's Office Scene
Strike—
Skewed contract

Newspaper with a stuffed envelope in its folds (Uncle Billy)
Zuzu's Bedroom
Preset—
Small bed with pink blanket
Artificial rose, its stem easily separated from blossom
Loose petals
Third Potter's Office Scene
Strike—
Uncle Billy's envelope

Insurance policy (George)
The Bridge
Preset—
Railing at Clarence's platform

ACT II

Bridgetender's house
Preset—
Clothesline with towels, some of Clarence's clothes and apparent
duplicates of George's clothes
Bench
Coffee mug
(Optional: small wood-burning stove)
The "House"
Preset—
Wagon with window frame hung with crimson curtains; wagon also
holds a small bar complete with bottle, glasses, bar-top bell and
hidden baseball bat
Blackjack (Bert)
Ma Bailey's

Preset—
Open doorway with identifying sign
Graveyard
Preset—
Three small "markers"
Library
Books, purse (Mary)
Second Bridge
Dime, petals (George)
Finale
Preset—
    Wagon with window frame hung with white curtains; wagon also holds dining room table (probably with chairs—but optional, depending on staging), the table set with several small glasses
Strike—
Bridge railing as scene begins

Purse with sheaf of banknotes (Mother)
Laundry basket filled with banknotes, a hidden wine bottle and Clarence's watch (Uncle Billy)
Cablegram (Gower)
A few dollars (Vi)
Large, decorated Christmas tree, ready to plug in (Bert and Potter's Man)
A roll of bills (Potter's Man)
A Christmas tree angel (Clarence)
(Note: There actually are Christmas tree angels which are easily plugged into a socket at the top of tree and light both brightly and immediately; it's a great effect if *easily* done.)

SOUND EFFECTS

Breaking glass
Train whistle
Crashing garbage cans
Pouring rain
Splash noises
Wind
Siren
Slamming car door
Gong (for Clarence's watch.)

SOME LIGHTING SUGGESTIONS

First Bridge Scene can be primarily lit by low-angle lights which project *up* toward George at such an angle as to place his shadow and the lattice-work of the bridge on the scrim. This bizarre and desperate effect can be initially repeated in Second Bridge Scene— but normal lighting must return after George's prayer (on the same cue that kills the Wind Effect), thus allowing time to roll in the wagon for the Finale.

(Note that it doesn't matter in First Bridge Scene if the low-angle lights partially illuminate Potter's Office where Potter remains frozen in his chair, or even Zuzu's Bedroom with the bed remaining onstage.)

Depending on space between the scrim and drop, footlights can be used behind the Lost Souls to project larger-than-life silhouettes onto the scrim. Perhaps the easiest way to silhouette them, however, is to backlight the Pottersville drop so that the only light in which they're seen comes through the drop before "projecting" their silhouettes onto the scrim.

COSTUME PLOT

Bearing in mind that the period is the 1930's and '40's:

GEORGE—except for After the Prom, in which he wears a too-large football jersey and pants—wears the same brown or gray suit throughout. In the First S&L Scene he adds a black armband— which is struck thereafter. He adds a fedora in Bailey Walk (and carries it in First Potter's Office Scene). His War Tableau accessories are described in the property plot. He adds a raincoat only for Money and Honeymoon, and a long, dark scarf in Search, which he continues to wear thereafter, concealing it and other clothing beneath a blanket and (optional) underwear "dickey" at Bridgetender's House.

MARY wears the same simple house dress in Opening and Finale, adding an apron only for Zuzu's Bedroom. She wears a long white terry-cloth robe with a trailing belt After the Prom ... a lovely, almost bride-like party dress in Wedding Reception ... a raincoat in Money... a modest but beautiful negligee and robe in Honeymoon ... a bright spring dress in Bailey Walk ... and in

Library: glasses, a mannish hat, sensible shoes, and a severe gray suit (its jacket long enough to suggest protection against the cold), her hair in a bun.

MOTHER wears a pretty, Christmasy dress in Opening/Finale ... another dress in S&L ... a pretty, if motherly, party dress at Wedding Reception ... her dress and hair style both frumpy at Ma Bailey's.

VIOLET wears a chic suit with with a small fur piece Opening/ Finale ... a skirt and blouse in S&L ... a gorgeous party dress at Wedding Reception ... a dazzling spring dress in Bailey Walk ... and an evening gown as crimson as the curtains at the House.

UNCLE BILLY, like George, wears the same suit throughout, removing his jacket for both S&L scenes, adding an overcoat and hat for only the Second Potter's Office Scene and Search.

ZUZU—except for Bailey Walk, in which she dresses as a boy with cap, short pants, etc.—wears the same flannel nightgown throughout.

BERT wears a suit at Wedding Reception, but is otherwise dressed as a policeman.

ERNIE wears a windbreaker and peaked cap in most of his scenes, removing the cap only for Wedding Reception (in which he wears a suitcoat and tie) and the House (in which he wears no coat or tie but adds sleeve garters).

MR. GOWER is spiffy in a shirt, tie, and white lab coat throughout—except for the House, in which he wears ill-fitting clothes, dirties his face and musses his hair.

MR. POTTER wears the same dark, richly textured suit throughout.

POTTER'S MAN wears a black suit, black tie, and stiff collar throughout.

HARRY wears a Navy pilot's uniform in Opening/Finale ... a shirt and tie in S&L ... and adds a suitcoat at Wedding Reception.

CLARENCE wears a pre-Revolutionary outfit throughout Act I which includes a ruffled-front shirt, knickers, long white stockings and buckled shoes. In Act II he wears a suit, tie, overcoat and fedora, all of the period. However, we briefly see his undershirt and it is far too long. His Finale costume is described below.

MISCELLANY

Ideally, two painted scrims will be used to accomplish the winter/summer tree effect, but it can also be done with one scrim, by flying a set of silhouetted trees while lowering the other—but flying both for the Lost Souls scenes.

Clarence's platform must be wide enough to accommodate George and Bert in Act II, and tall enough so that Clarence can easily put the angel atop the tree. The bridge railing should be operated by remote control ropes so that it can readily be popped into place and as readily struck.

Regarding Potter's wheelchair: It is, of course, the tall, old-fashioned kind, and his constant property throughout Act I. In Act II—as one of the Lost Souls, he is best seated on a stool facing partially away from the audience so as to not be easily recognized.

Regarding Clarence's wings: Perhaps the best way to mount them is to fit the actor with a harness (the wings already attached), which is worn *under* his flowing robe, the robe carefully slit in two places to accommodate the wings.

The wings themselves are made of two pieces of tubing, each bent to resemble an inverted U, covered with white cloth, and hung with mesh—to which is sewn overlapping white cloth panels. Each panel, about eight inches tall and three inches wide, is attached at the top only and curved on the corners that show. From any distance these panels remarkably resemble long white feathers and react like feathers as he moves. The effect is truly seraphic, promoting sustained applause as Clarence makes his final, crossover entrance.

FAVORITE MUSICALS *from*

"The House of Plays"

A FINE AND PRIVATE PLACE

(**All Groups**) Book & Lyrics by Erik Haagensen. Music by Richard Isen. Adapted from the novel by Peter S. Beagle. 3m., 2f, (may be played by 2m., 2f.) + 1 raven (may be either m. or f.) Ext. setting. "The grave's a fine and private place,/But none, I think, do there embrace." Little did you know, Andrew Marvell, that someday, someone would come up with a charming love story, set in a graveyard, about two lost souls who are buried there, who meet and fall in love. Also inhabiting the cemetery is an eccentric old man who has the gift of being able to see and converse with the inhabitants of the graves, as well as with a raven who swoops in at mealtimes with some dinner he has swiped for the old guy. Also present from time to time is a delightful old Jewish widow, whose husband Morris is buried in the cemetery. She often stops by to tell Morris what's new. Her name is Gertrude, and it is soon apparent that she also stops by to flirt with old Jonathan Rebeck (she doesn't know he actually *lives* there). A crisis arises when it appears the young couple will be separated. The young man, it seems, has been deemed a suicide and, as such, he must be removed from consecrated ground. Their only hope is Jonathan; but to help them Jonathan must come out in the open. Had we but world enough, and time, we would tell you how Jonathan manages to salvage the romance; but we'll just have to hope the above story intrigues you enough to examine the delightful libretto and wonderfully tuneful music for yourself. A sell-out, smash hit at the Goodspeed in Connecticut and, later, at the American Stage Co. in New Jersey (the professional theatre which premiered *Other People's Money),* this happy, whimsical, sentimental, up-beat new show will delight audiences of all ages. .   (**#8154**)

NEW FROM SAMUEL FRENCH, INC.

SMOKE ON THE MOUNTAIN
Musical
All Groups

Book by Constance Ray. Conceived by Alan Bailey. Music & lyrics by various authors. 4m., 3f. Int. setting. Imagine a combination of *Pump Boys and Dinettes* and *Talking With* if you want to know about this daffy, delightful new show. We are at the Mt. Pleasant (North Carolina) Baptist Church in 1938, at a Saturday Night Gospel Sing arranged by Pastor Mervin Oglethorpe, a young and enthusiastic minister who also works part time in the local pickle factory, who very cautiously wants to bring his congregation into the "modern world" by (gasp!) having a concert in church! Clearly, many of the, shall we say, "less-square" members of the congregation (us in the audience) think this is a swell idea; but not Miss Maude and Miss Myrtle, two elderly spinsters who are the church's chief benefactors, who are in attendance to make sure nobody enjoys themselves. The evening's entertainment is provided by the Sanders Family Gospel Singers, who perform a slew of standard bluegrass gospel songs, from "Church in the Wildwood" to "I'm Using My Bible As a Roadmap." Between songs, the family members "witness" by telling personal stories—some quirkily humorous and others downright moving—that relate to their trials of faith. A huge success at the McCarter Theatre in Princeton (where it won over even our cynical Editor), *Smoke on the Mountain* was subsequently successfully produced in New York by the Lambs Theatre. "Wildly funny . . . so well-written is this [show] that, instead of laughing at it, I found myself laughing with it, rooting for the family, and singing along and clapping with the rest of the audience. *Smoke on the Mountain* reaches out and grabs you."—The Trentonian. "Exhilarating! A rollicking blend of monologues and musical numbers that adds up to a compone *Chorus Line*."—Variety. "A sophisticated audience went simply wild over *Smoke on the Mountain*."—Philadelphia Daily News. "A charming and funny celebration of Americana. With its mixture of softened cracker-barrel humor, Christian sweetness and light, and its attitude of gentle amusement at the squareness of it all, *Smoke on the Mountain* creates the same mood, at once sentimental and whimsical, [as] *Pump Boys and Dinettes*."—N.Y. Times. (#21236)

Other Publications for Your Interest

MAIL
(ADVANCED GROUPS—MUSICAL)
Book & Lyrics by JERRY COLKER
Music by MICHAEL RUPERS

9 men, 6 women—2 Sets

What a terrific idea for a "concept musical"! As *Mail* opens Alex, an unpublished novelist, is having an acute anxiety attack over his lack of success in writing and his indecision regarding his girlfriend, Dana; so, he "hits the ground running" and doesn't come back for 4 months! When Alex finally returns to his apartment, he finds an unending stream of messages on his answering machine and stacks and stacks of unopened mail. As he opens his mail, it in effect comes to life, as we learn what has been happening with Alex's friends, and with Dana, during his absence. There is also some hilarious junk mail, which bombards Alex muscially, as well as unpaid bills from the likes of the electric company (the ensemble comes dancing out of Alex's refrigerator singing "We're Gonna Turn Off Your Juice"). In the second act, we move into a sort of abstract vision of Alex's world, a blank piece of paper upon which he can, if he is able, and if he wishes, start over—with his writing, with his friends, with his father and, maybe, with Dana. Producers looking for something wild and crazy will, we know, want to open *this* MAIL, a hit with audiences and critics coast-to-coast, from the authors of THREE GUYS NAKED FROM THE WAIST DOWN! "At least 12 songs are solid enough to stand on their own. If MAIL can't deliver, there is little hope for the future of the musical theatre, unless we continue to rely on the British to take possession of a truly American art form."—Drama-Logue. "Make room for the theatre's newest musical geniuses."—The Same. (Terms quoted on application. Music available on rental. See p. 48.)

(#15199)

CHESS
(ADVANCED GROUPS—MUSICAL/OPERA)
Book by RICHARD NELSON
Lyrics by TIM RICE
Music by BJORN ULVAEUS & BENNY ANDERSSON

9 men, 2 women, 1 female child, plus ensemble

A *musical* about an *international chess match?!?!* A bad idea from the get-go, you'd think; but no—Tim Rice (he of *Evita, Joseph and the Amazing Technicolor Dreamcoat* and *Jesus Christ Superstar*), Bjorn Ulvaeus and Benny Andersson (they of Swedish Supergroup ABBA) and noted American playwright Richard Nelson, all in collaboration with Trevor Nunn (*Les Miz., Nick Nick*, etc.) have pulled it off, creating an extraordinary rock opera about international intrigue which uses as a metaphor a media-drenched chess match between a loutish American champion (shades of Bobby Fischer) and a nice-guy Soviet champion. The American has a girlfriend, Florence, there in Bangkok (where the match takes place) to be his second and to provide moral support. There she meets, and falls in love with, Anatoly, the Soviet champion—and the sparks fly, particularly when Anatoly decides to defect to the west, causing a postponement and change of venue to Budapest. Eventually, it is clear that all the characters are merely pawns in a larger chess match between the C.I.A. and the KGB! The pivotal role of Florence is perhaps the most extra-ordinary and complex role in the musical theatre since Eva Peron; and the roles of Freddie and Anatoly (both tenors) are great, too. Several of the songs have become international hits, including Florence's "Heaven Help My Heart", "I know Him So Well" and "Nobody's On Nobody's Side", and Freddie's descent into the maelstrom of decadence, "One Night in Bangkok". Playing to full houses and standing ovations, *Chess* closed exceedingly prematurely on Broadway; and, perhaps the story behind *that* just might make the basis of another Rice/ABBA/Nelson/Nunn collaboration! (Terms quoted on application. Music available on rental. See p. 48.) Slightly restricted.

(#5236)

Other Publications for Your Interest

THE BEST CHRISTMAS PAGEANT EVER
(ALL GROUPS—CHRISTMAS COMEDY)
By BARBARA ROBINSON

4 men, 6 women, 8 boys, 9 girls—2 Interiors

Looking for an alternative this Christmas to the old, traditional, Joseph-Mary-and-the-Three Wise-Men Christmas play? Look no further: here is *The Best Christmas Pageant Ever*! The hilarious story concerns the efforts of a woman and her husband to put on the annual church Christmas pageant despite having to cast the Herdman kids—probably the meanest, nastiest, most inventively awful kids in the history of the world. You won't believe the mayhem—and the fun—when the Herdmans meet the Christmas story in a head-on collision! "An American classic."—McCall's Magazine. "One of the best Christmas stories ever—and certainly one of the funniest."—Seattle Times. A recent sell-out hit in Seattle, this delightful comedy is ideal for all groups. It is adapted from the only story ever to run twice in McCall's Magazine, and Avon has over 800,000 copies of the original story in print. (#248)

A CHRISTMAS CAROL
(CHRISTMAS PLAY)
By MICHAEL PALLER

5 men, 2 women, 3 children—Composite set

Adapted by Michael Paller from Charles Dickens' story. A fresh approach to the classic tale while still faithfully preserving Dickens' magic. At Dickens' home, Christmas Eve 1843, his family and friends ask him to tell them a story but he refuses. It's Christmas—after all—and you can't expect a man to work on Christmas eve. No—he has a different idea. If there's going to be a story—let them each take a part in its telling. And so the story of Scrooge, Marley, the Cratchits and all unfolds. The cast of ten plays over forty parts. "Done with both respect and ingenuity. Deserves to be seen."—Cleveland Press. "A treat, A play-within-a-play that works wonderfully. Could become an annual holiday piece for the whole family to enjoy."—Cleveland Sun Press. (#5100)